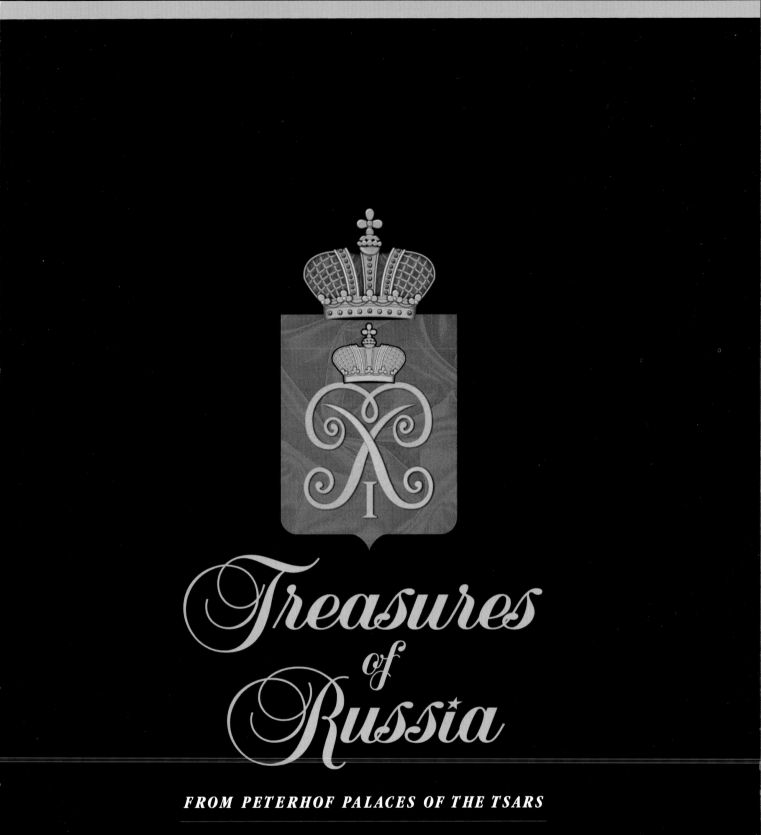

Treasures
of
Russia

FROM PETERHOF PALACES OF THE TSARS

Catalog of the Exhibit - Published on the occasion of the exhibition, Treasures of Russia from Peterhof, which was made possible by the Rio Suite Hotel & Casino and the The State Museum Reserve -Peterhof and organized by Encore Entertainment Group, Inc.

Photography Credits - Reproductions of the objects in the exhibition are by permission of the lenders. Lending institutions supplied the color transparencies; additional photography credits follow: The State Museum Reserve -"Peterhof"; The Forbes Magazine Collection, New York; A La Vieille Russie, New York and the Rio Suite Hotel & Casino.

Treasures of Russia

FROM PETERHOF PALACES OF THE TSARS

Presented by:

Rio All-Suite Casino Resort

The State Museum Reserve - Peterhof

Encore Entertainment Group, Inc.

Major Sponsors:

 **Bank of America**

Bernard K Passman G A L L E R Y

Sponsor:

NEVADA BEVERAGE C O M P A N Y

Audio tours provided by:

A N T E N N A U D I O
Salsalito, California

Advertising partner:

Special thanks:

Marnell Corrao Associates
Providing construction and interiors services,
Las Vegas, Nevada

A. A. Marnell, Chartered
Providing architectural services,
Las Vegas, Nevada

Front Cover: Night View of The Great Palace at Peterhof and The Great Cascade. *Pages 2-3:* View of The Great Palace at Peterhof and The Great Cascade. *Page 6:* The Great Cascade: The "Samson Rendering Open the Jaws of the Lion" Fountain. *Page 8:* The Great Cascade *Page 10:* Imperial Chanticleer Egg from the FORBES Magazine Collection, New York. (page 102) *Page 12:* The Adaro Foundation. *Page 15:* The Catherine Wing. *Page 18:* The Great Cascade: The Basket Foundation. *Page 94:* The Marriage Cup courtesy of A LA VIEILLE RUSSIE, New York. *Page 116:* The Great Palace and The Great Cascade. (page 124)

Contents

Catalogue of the Exhibit

— • —

Published on the occasion of the exhibition "TREASURES OF RUSSIA" from Peterhof,
which was made possible by The State Museum Reserve-"Peterhof" and the Rio Suite Hotel & Casino,
and organized through Encore Entertainment Group, Inc.

*Author of the concept of the exhibit
and scientific editor of the Catalogue*
Nina Vernova

Paintings and drawings
Nina Vernova

Sculpture
Vil' Yumangulov

Rare books
Marina Trubanovskaya

Archives
Tatiana Litvina

Precious metals and metals
Nina Vernova

Porcelain and glass
Tamara Nosovich

Furniture
Elena Gerasimenko

Fabrics
Marina Kaznakova

Photography
Alexander Ivanov

Translation
Michael Wasserman
Dale Pesmen

Catalogue Coordination
Rio Suite Hotel & Casino

Catalogue Manager
Dianne Millier

Publisher
Forbes Custom Publishing,
New York

Lenders

— • —

The State Museum Reserve-"Peterhof"
St. Petersburg, Russia

The Forbes Magazine Collection
New York, New York

A La Vieille Russie
New York, New York

Foreword

— • —

I am pleased to welcome you to the exhibition "TREASURES OF RUSSIA" from Peterhof. The palace-museums and park at Peterhof are known throughout the world. Each year more than six million guests visit the three parks and ten museums of this architectural complex.

The construction of Peterhof began in 1705. Over the course of two centuries it was constantly expanded and enriched. The finest architects of Russia, the most prominent artists, sculptors, and masters of the decorative and applied arts made their contributions to the founding and flourishing of this gem of world culture.

During the Second World War, in 1941–1945, for 900 days, Peterhof was occupied by the German Nazis and entirely destroyed.

It took decades for its internationally renowned collection to rise from the ashes.

Today Peterhof figures on the UNESCO list of monuments of world culture and has the status of a Treasure of Russia. It is the only monarch's residence in the world to have been built on the shore of a sea. Every year, every day from May to October, all of its 150 fountains and three splendid cascades are in operation. Almost every year, during the summer season, new palaces and pavilions, freshly restored, open to the public.

During the Second World War, the majority of Peterhof's collections were evacuated deeper into Russia's interior, and were thus saved. But much was destroyed and looted by the occupying German Nazis.

For this reason, over the last decades, the museum has conducted an active search for objects which once graced the halls of these palaces, as well as for similar specimens to replace them.

Daily, new objects, including many obtained at auctions at Sotheby's and Christie's, are added to the museums' collections.

But of particular importance are those objects that actually witnessed so many historical events of utmost importance for Russia, Europe, and the entire world. Many of them remember Peter the Great, his daughter Elizabeth Petrovna, Catherine II's accession to the throne, Alexander I, victor over Napoleon Bonaparte, Nicholas I, the Tsar-reformer Alexander II, and the last Tsar, Nicholas II. Incidentally, it was here at Peterhof that his children, the heir to the throne Alexei and daughters Tatiana, Maria, and Anastasia, who is still spoken of today, were born and spent their childhood years.

Peterhof, with its opulent palaces, its gold sculptures gleaming in the sun, the silver streams of its fountains, and its air laced by the sea, is one of the most joyous places on our planet.

The collections of this State Museum Reserve are often exhibited in Europe and Asia. They have been displayed in the United States as well.

But this is the first time in history that such a vast number of objects is leaving Peterhof, and it is in order to lend its magnificence to an exposition across the ocean, in the city of Las Vegas.

Thank you for your interest in Russian history and culture. I hope that this exhibit will bring you pleasure and acquaint you with yet another page in the book of Russian art.

Vadim Znamenov
General Director
The State Museum Reserve
"Peterhof"

Imperial Chanticleer Egg

Preface

—·—

The Rio Suite Hotel & Casino is extremely proud and honored to bring the "Treasures of Russia" to the United States and to the State of Nevada. This event is truly an historic and cultural exchange between nations. Hosting an exhibit of this caliber creates an unprecedented opportunity to expose the beauty of the incredible epic story of the Romanov dynasty to guests and visitors from throughout the world.

Indeed, such a program provides a tremendous educational opportunity for the students in Nevada to experience history first-hand. We would like to extend our sincere thanks to Governor Bob Miller and the State of Nevada for their enthusiastic efforts in supporting this unique educational experience.

Since opening in 1990, the Rio has been recognized as a leader and innovator in the resort industry for its commitment to provide the very best to its guests. Adding this once-in-a-lifetime exhibit, the Rio once again sets the standard. The "Treasures of Russia" stands as a testament of the Rio's dedication to the arts and to our continual quest to provide the best in the most innovative ways.

I know that you will find this display of art as moving and as inspiring as I do.

Anthony A. Marnell, II
Chairman and CEO
Rio Suite Hotel & Casino

Introduction

—·—

The historical, cultural and educational significance of the "Treasures of Russia" Exhibition from The State Museum Reserve-Peterhof allows our two countries a wonderful opportunity to forge a bond. Our Exhibition will contribute to a greater understanding of our cultures and we will have a better appreciation of each other's heritage.

Peterhof is a treasure to people from all over the world. Its beautiful parks, fountains and palaces represent the most artistically splendid periods of Russian history. Constructed by Peter the Great and occupied by his descendants, this famous Park and Museum is admired by millions annually, and is a major part of Russian and world history from Peter the Great (1725) to Nicholas II (1918).

"Treasures of Russia" is the largest Russian exhibition ever presented (showcasing more than twelve hundred objects); and is the result of the talents, dedication and hard work of many. I want to thank and express my sincere gratitude to Dr. Vadim V. Znamenov, General Director, and Ms. Nina V. Vernova, Vice Director of The State Museum Reserve-Peterhof and their entire staff for their many months of dedicated work that made this outstanding Exhibition possible.

A special thanks go out to Anthony A. Marnell II, Chairman and Chief Executive Officer of Rio Suite Hotel & Casino, and David P. Hanlon, for having the vision to host this first ever, world-class exhibition held in Las Vegas, Nevada. Without their firm commitment this Exhibition on the West Coast of America would not have been possible.

A special note of appreciation must be extended to Paul and Mark Schaffer of A La Vieille Russie, Inc. in New York City for their generous loan, which included ten beautiful Fabergé pieces. We also thank "Kip" Forbes and Mrs. Margaret Kelly Trombly, Director of the Forbes Magazine Collection, for their loan of the magnificent "Imperial Chanticleer Egg".

Our curator efforts have been exceptional; I would like to express particular appreciation to Ms. Dianne M. Millier, Russia Curator Liaison, and Mrs. Tamara Nosovich, Chief Curator of Peterhof for their tireless and endless months of work to produce this exhibit in America. And to Lee Cagley, Director of Interior Design for Marnell Corrao Associates, who designed and re-created some of the most beautiful settings and room interiors of Peterhof Museum for our exhibit.

Finally, to Thomas A. Roberts, our very talented staff at Encore, and to our excellent team of volunteers, I express my deepest appreciation for your contributions.

Robert C. Nargassans
Managing Director "Treasures of Russia" and President of Encore Entertainment Group, Inc.

History of Peterhof—The Summer Capital of the Russian Emperors

Peterhof is the oldest country residence of the Russian tsars near Petersburg. From the time it was founded by Peter the Great (Peter the First) at the beginning of the 18th century, more than ten palaces were erected here, graceful garden-park pavilions were built, and a unique system of waterworks was created, allowing close to one hundred and fifty fountains to adorn the parks of the Emperor's residence. The Great Cascade, sparkling with the gleam of its powerful streams of water and gold sculptures, is a fantastic spectacle.

The uninterrupted construction of new palaces, fountains, and parks continued for two centuries. During its years of existence a colossal wealth of cultural valuables was amassed at Peterhof. Its parks were adorned by excellent sculptures; its palaces, built according to the plans of prominent architects, became the focus of a remarkable collection of paintings, art furniture, bronzes, porcelain, and glass. Almost every one of the rulers found it necessary to make his or her contribution to the decoration of Peterhof, which played the role of the summer capital of Russia. The best architects, sculptors, painters, and masters of decorative and applied arts in the gigantic Empire, both native and invited from many countries of Europe, joined their names and fates with those of Peterhof.

The residence of the Romanovs became the site of historical events which had an influence not only on the destiny of Russia but on those of many other countries of the world.

Construction on the shore of the Gulf of Finland began in 1705, and the ceremonial opening of Peterhof took place in August 1723. The first fountains flung their streams high into the air; the doors of the Upper Halls (the future Great Palace) and the Monplaisir and Marly Palaces were thrown open, and construction of the Hermitage Pavilion, the first Hermitage in Russia, was in full swing.

By that time the "Russian Versailles" had already stunned foreign guests. The French minister at the Russian court, the Marquis de Campredon, in his report to the King on his visit to Peterhof "together with other foreign ministers," did not hide his delight with all that he had seen: "The Tsar met us on the shore of a canal leading from the sea to the palace. This canal is straight, 1000 steps in length and 20 in width, is faced with stone and equipped with locks which are excellently suited for the entrance and exit of flotillas...a splendid fountain adorned...by gilded figures supplies it with water."

The erection of "Peterhof," which in translation from Dutch meant "Peter's Court," began on the shores of the Gulf of Finland with the Monplaisir Palace. Its basic design was defined by Peter the Great himself. The Emperor indicated the location of the palace, its layout, and even some elements of its decoration.

The principal noteworthy feature of Monplaisir was its gallery of pictures, collected by Peter I himself. It counts among its collections canvases by Dutch and Flemish, as well as some Italian, German, and other masters. Even at the time, many foreign guests appreciated the collection as being "of highly good merit."

The twenty years during which Peter the First's niece, Anna Ioannovna, ruled over the Russian throne were not the brightest years in the history of Russia. Peterhof, however, continued to be the ceremonial summer residence, and the Empress did much towards its maintenance and improvement. She fulfilled many ideas of Peter the Great that the founder of the capital of fountains did not have time to realize. Under Anna Ioannovna were built the Samson fountain (which later became the symbol of Peterhof), twenty-two fountains along the canal leading to the Gulf of Finland, the Cascade of Dragons (later known as Chessboard Mountain), as well as the two Rome Fountains. The construction of the Golden Mountain Cascade was completed.

Anna Ioannovna spent the better part of her summers at Peterhof. Her life here was not particularly varied: she rose at 7:00 in the morning, lunched at 12, and went to sleep at 9. Her principal entertainment was hunting. At the site where a later Emperor, Nicholas I, would build Alexandria Park, the Empress assembled a sizeable menagerie in which buffalo, boars, and even tigers were kept.

Until the present day a lacquered panel from the wall trimming of the Chinese Study of Monplaisir Palace can be found in the collection of the Peterhof museums. The panel has bullets in it which were shot from Empress Anna Ioannovna's gun during a deer hunt. Sometimes the Empress would entertain herself by shooting at birds directly from the balcony of the Great Palace. For this purpose loaded firearms always stood both on the balcony and in the rooms.

The most festive occasion at Peterhof at that time was the ball for the Preobrazhensky Regiment, the regiment founded by Peter the Great.

From the moment of the accession to the throne of the Empress Elizabeth Petrovna, life at Peterhof changed. The daughter of Peter the First worshiped the memory of her father and imitated him in many ways. She inherited his passion for collecting and for building new palaces. During her rule the modest dimensions of the Petrine constructions were significantly enlarged, and the Peterhof collections continued to grow. It was precisely at this time that the court architect, F. B. Rastrelli, transformed Peter's Upper Halls into the magnificent Great Palace, erected the Catherine Wing of Monplaisir, and drew up plans for new fountains. Elizabeth's splendid court called for

vast and rich palaces as well as magnificent parks, where brilliantly elegant balls and firework displays were staged, amazing European monarchs.

Balls took place almost every day. Diaries of chamber officers chronicled them: people gathered at six o'clock in the evening, danced and played cards until ten. Then the Empress, along with a circle of privileged individuals, sat down to supper. The rest of the invited guests dined standing. The Empress Elizabeth surprised everyone by her appetite and her open passion for cabbage soup, boiled salted pork, meat pie, and buckwheat kasha. At Shrovetide she would eat up to two dozen *bliny*, crepe-like Russian pancakes, which practice drove her physician to distraction.

State dinners with invited foreign ambassadors and guests followed more complicated systems of ceremonies and of seating arrangements at table, which were based on individuals' class and rank. The menu would be refined, as befit such dinners. Examples of dishes served at the Royal table might be: "Soup of Little Cheeks of Herring;" "'Awakening in the Morn' Beef Eyes in Sauce;" "Beef Palate in Ash with Truffles;" "Goose in Shoes," etc. The soups alone were served in five or six courses, so dinners usually lasted several hours. Such dinners were served by an enormous staff consisting of more than 500 people. Musical accompaniment made these dinners even more noisy and festive.

Thus lived the court of Elizabeth, the daughter of the founder of Peterhof.

In 1762 Peterhof became the site of an important historical event, which for many years determined Russia's path. On June 28th of that year the Grand Duchess Catherine Alexeevna secretly left Peterhof in order to raise the elite regiments of guards at Petersburg, depose her spouse Peter III, and become the Empress to be known later by the name of Catherine the Great.

The reigning "country squire," as she liked to call herself, did not bestow on Peterhof any particular favor; it awakened in her too many unpleasant memories of her former life in the court of Elizabeth. Nevertheless, though she spent her summers in Tsarskoe Selo, Catherine paid homage to the founder of the summer residence and did not forget Peterhof. She usually came here for Peter's name day, which she celebrated magnificently. Here, also, the maritime victories over the Turks were celebrated. Catherine was also drawn here when she "wanted to rest from the endless labors and noisy court life." Here, in the words of Catherine herself, she "led the most simple lifestyle: rose at 6 o'clock, took a walk around the Lower Gardens; at 8 o'clock took coffee on the terrace of Monplaisir…and read a great deal…to rid myself of boredom."

Unlike her predecessor, Catherine the Second was indifferent to food, never overate, and fasted twice a week, on Wednesdays and Fridays. Her dinner lasted about an hour. The dishes were very simple. The favorite dish of the Empress was boiled beef with salted pickles; her favorite drink was water with currant syrup; she also drank, by doctor's orders, a glass of madeira and rhine wine. For dessert she partook of fruits, primarily apples and cherries.

What Catherine had true passion for was extremely strong black coffee. She began her day with it.

Six o'clock in the evening was the time for cards. The Empress played "vint at ten rubles per round, rocambole, piquet or boston." She played well and did not like losing. If she lost, she did not become angry, but she always made a loser pay up. The games ended by ten o'clock. At night she drank only a glass of boiled water and went to bed. This is how her day ended.

Under Catherine the Great, construction, for which the Empress herself admitted a passion, extended to Peter's beloved creation. During her reign the Lower Park and many interiors of the Great Palace changed their appearance, but most importantly, Peterhof's borders expanded beyond those established by its founder. By Catherine's commission, the architect G. Quarenghi built the renowned English Palace in the English (not only in name but in design) Park.

An avid collector, Catherine poured all her enthusiasm into founding the Hermitage Museum in Petersburg, while, at the same time, not neglecting the summer residence. It was at this time that significant

works of the Imperial Porcelain Factory, Russian artists' bronzes, splendid chandeliers, and silks from France appeared at Peterhof. The portrait gallery was expanded.

The Emperor Paul the First, though he did not respect his mother particularly highly, jealously revered the memory of his great-grandfather, and considered it his duty to take care of Peterhof. During the years of his rule new fountains appeared in the parks of Peter the Great, old fountains were renovated, and the sculptures of the Great Cascade, having become dilapidated, were replaced. For these grandiose endeavors the best sculptors of Russia, from the Petersburg Academy of Arts, I. Kozlovsky, F. Shubin, F. Shchedrin, I. Prokofiev, and I. Martos, were recruited.

The son of Paul Petrovich, Alexander I, continued the work of his father, despite the fact that he spent the better part of his reign outside the borders of Russia, on military campaigns and travels abroad. Among other things, he replaced the statues of the fountains in the Monplaisir gardens and had colonnades erected in front of the Great Cascade. But perhaps the most important impact left on Peterhof during the twelve-year rule of the grandson of Catherine the Great was the significant enrichment of the palaces by works of art. These came from his father's acquisitions for the Mikhailov Castle and purchases in Europe, diplomatic gifts, and simply gifts from intimates. Maria Feodorovna, the wife of Paul I, loved her personal estate, Pavlovsk, more than she did Peterhof, though she, like the others, honored the "Court of Peter," and thus, in her will, bequeathed many objects to Peterhof.

During the reign of Alexander I, the famous traditional Peterhof festival, which attained nearly worldwide fame and was described in many works of literature, was born. Annually, on June 22nd, on the name day of the widowed Empress and mother of the conqueror of Napoleon Bonaparte, countless numbers of people streamed from the capital and its environs towards Peterhof to marvel at the magnificent illuminations and fireworks.

With the accession to the throne of Nicholas I, Peterhof underwent a rebirth. Honoring the memory of his illustrious great-grandfather and, in certain respects, worshipping him, the Emperor did everything possible to preserve and magnify what Peter had be-

gun. He made the Peterhof residence his primary summer abode.

While still Grand Duke, Nicholas began construction east of the Lower Gardens. The "Alexandria" Park was created and, according to designs by architect A. Menelaus, the gothic-style "Cottage" Palace, a farm, and the Court church, the Capella, were built. Having inherited from his grandmother Catherine II a passion for building, the grandson of the great Empress expanded the territory of Peterhof by several times, filling it with the most varied structures.

Nicholas I also continued and added to what his brother had begun: the family festivals were celebrated in previously unheard-of splendor. The yearly illuminations on the 1st and 22nd of June, on the birthdays and name days of Alexandra Feodorovna, wife of the reigning Emperor, and of Maria Feodorovna, outshone by contrast everything of the sort that had been done before. The Lower Park served as the center of the illumination: "…innumerable multicolored fires adorned the green of the trees, flower beds, and flowering bushes; glowing arcs of light were thrown over the Samson Canal, and chandeliers of lanterns illuminated the Monplaisir gardens. Magnificent fireworks were set off on board boats standing in the waterway. During the illumination, at the Palace, a masquerade was held…attendance by the public was such that for days before the festivities it was impossible in Petersburg to procure either a horse-drawn cab and driver or a ticket on a boat going in that direction."

Nicholas I did so much for Peterhof that changes made during the following Tsar's reign are not always noticed. Nevertheless, "the Court of Peter" was never ignored: throughout the 19th century extensive restoration was undertaken on the Great Cascade and on areas of the Lower Park. Reconstruction and repairs were also executed on certain structures of Alexandria, and much was changed in other parks on the Peterhof Palace Complex.

The last Russian Emperor, Nicholas II, paid special attention to Peterhof. Like Peter, he was drawn to the sea. Therefore it is not by chance that it was on the shore of the Gulf of Finland that a palace, the Lower Dacha, was built for him. This completed the construction of palaces at Peter's residence. Nicholas the Second spent almost the entire summer there. As the

Tsar's children's teacher, Pierre Gilliard, recalled, the Tsar "shared his ancestors' preference for the enchanting place that is Peterhof. Each summer he came here with his family and settled in the small dacha at Alexandria, surrounded by the shady park." The Emperor's journal is teeming with joyful memories of days lived here. His children Tatiana, Maria, Anastasia, and Alexei were born here and christened in the palace Church of Peter and Paul.

And, despite a certain degree of decline in interest in Peterhof during the reigns of Alexander II and his son, it was, even then, the ceremonial summer residence: here official representatives of foreign governments were received, here the day of holy Peter was observed, as were the name days, birthdays, weddings and betrothals of the imperial family. In short, Peterhof was always felt to be a place that could not harbor tears or sadness, a place of perennial celebration.

In the second half of the 19th century and the beginning of the 20th alone Peterhof's famous palaces and parks were visited by: the German Emperor Wilhelm the Second; the King of Denmark, Christian the Fourth; the Italian King Umberto; the Khans of Khiva and Bukhara; the Emperor of Brazil; the President of France, R. Poincare; the rulers of all the Balkan kingdoms and princedoms, etc. Particularly noteworthy were the festivities marking the 1894 wedding day of the Grand Duchess Ksenia Alexandrovna and those in 1897 in honor of the visit of French president Felix Faure.

Even after a revolution and a war had stormed over the summer residence of the Russian Emperors, Peterhof, and though far from all its wounds have been healed, it remains a symbol of the majesty of Russian culture. Today millions of visitors come from far and wide to marvel at this, one of the wonders of the world.

Nina Vernova
Vice-director
The State Museum Reserve
"Peterhof"

LOWER PARK

The LOWER PARK is the central palace-park ensemble of Peterhof residences. It became world renowned for its many, varied, deep fountains and cascades, and for its wealth of decorative gilded sculptures.

Created during the period 1714–1723 with the participation of architects J.-B. LeBlond, N. Michetti, and J. Braunstein, sculptor C. Rastrelli, and garden master L. Harnigfeld. Designed in a "regular" (French) style on a waterfront location and bordered on the southern side by a high natural terrace. Area: 102.5 hectares.

The center of the composition is the Great Palace on the summit of the terrace. At the base of the palace, cut into the slope of the hill, is the Great Cascade, a grandiose complex comprising 64 fountains and three waterfalls. The cascade is adorned by 255 works of decorative art, including 37 gilded bronze statues and groups. The ensemble of the Great Cascade includes the largest fountain of Peterhof, with jets of water reaching a height of 20 meters, as well as a monumental sculptural group, "Samson Tearing the Lion's Mouth."

A canal is laid from the Great Cascade to the sea, dividing the park into western and eastern halves. In the western half of the park are situated Peter I's palace, Marly, and the Hermitage Pavilion, the first Hermitage of Russia; in the eastern half of the park are Monplaisir Palace and Catherine's compound.

The park's decorative water appointments consist of 144 fountains and 4 cascades.

~ 1 ~

VASE

1995.
Copy of the 1800 original.

Warsaw, Poland.

"Art Braz"

Original: Petersburg, Russia, Casting House
of the Academy of Arts.

Architect A. Voronikhin and sculptor M. Kozlovsky, inspired by
an antique original of the 1st century A.D.

Bronze, gilding, coloring.

H. 101 cm.

Inv. No. PDMP 1069-sk

This vase-urn is decorated with plant and ram's head ornaments, and figures of a winged lion, a snow leopard, and griffins. It was executed according to a marble original of 1st century Roman origin preserved in the collection of the Imperial Hermitage. The vase was acquired by Catherine II in 1787 as part of the collection of English banker Lyde Browne.

By order of Emperor Paul I, in 1799–1806 the Academy of Arts undertook a major renovation of the Great Cascade decor. Deteriorating lead sculpture was replaced by bronze, and four types of decorative vases were created for the balustrades of the Great Cascade.

~ 2 ~

VASE

1995.
Copy of the 1800 original.

Warsaw, Poland.

"Art Braz"

Original: Petersburg, Russia, Casting House
of the Academy of Arts.

Architect A. Voronikhin and sculptor M. Kozlovsky,
after an antique original of the 2nd century A. D.

Bronze, gilding, coloring.

H. 89 cm.

Inv. No. PDMP 1071-sk

The handles are executed in the form of double swan's heads and terminate at the top in two-sided Bacchic female figures.

The original marble crater vase was discovered in an excavation at the Villa Adriana in Tivoli, near Rome.

—— 3 ——

STATUE "NYMPH"

1856.

Petersburg, Russia.

Saint Petersburg Maximilan Leuchtenberg Galvanoplastic,
Casting, and Mechanical Plant.

Copy of antique original of the 3rd century B.C.

Copper, casting, gilding.

H. 156 cm.

Inv. No. PDMP 235/1-sk

One of the appointments of a fountain of the same name. According to antique mythology, nymphs personified various natural elements. The ancients believed that the gurgling of water, identified with the speech of nymphs, could predict human fates. The marble original of this statue is in the collection of the State Hermitage. A galvanoplastic, gilded copy was created for the fountain, executed according to the design of architect A. I. Stakenshneider in 1853–1856.

ROMANOV GALLERY

Peter I (The Great)

—•—

Peter I (The Great) Alexeevich (1672–1725). Son of the Tsar Alexei Mikhailovich and his second wife, Natalia Naryshkina. He acceded to the throne in 1682. Tsar from 1698. First Russian Emperor from 1721.

— 4 —

PORTRAIT OF PETER I (THE GREAT)

1750s.

Unknown Russian Artist.

Copy from Godfrey Kneller (1646?–1723)

Oil on canvas.

146 × 113.5 cm.

Inv. No. PDMP 976-zh.

⇀ 5 ⇀
THRONE
1720–1725

Russia.

Oak, carving, gilding, fabric, velvet,
silver stitching.

H. 178 cm.

Inv. No. PDMP 360-mb

Gilded, with the imperial crown on the
summit of the back; armrests supported
by figures of griffins, a symbol of the Romanov line; lion faces (symbol of strong
power) on the corners of the seat, becoming legs in the form of lion paws.

According to legend, this armchair was
commissioned by the first general–governor of Petersburg, A.D. Menshikov, for a reception for Peter the First at his Great
Palace in Oranienbaum, a suburb of Petersburg located not far from Peterhof.

FOOTSTOOL FOR THRONE
1741–1750

Russia.

Linden wood, carving, gilding, velvet, gold galloon.

H. 28 cm.

Inv. No. PDMP 171-mb

Decorated with gilded carving in the form of flowers,
scrolls, and rocaille shell ornament.

⇀ 6 ⇀
SHIP SUNDIAL-CLOCK
1715.

London, England.

Rowley, John, 1674–1719.

Silver, copper, chasing, engraving, glass.

H. 45 cm.

Inscription on the clock face: "By His Majesty
Great Britain Command," "Made by J. Rowley
Master of Mechanicks to His Majesty."

Inv. No. PDMP 505-dm

On a round base with compass; on the surface of the
clock ring—a mirrored monogram of the English King
George the First: "GP" under a crown.

The clock was made by order from the English
King George the First and presented to Peter I as a
diplomatic gift.

7

MODEL OF A SMALL BOAT
BELONGING TO PETER THE FIRST

1754.

Petersburg

Craftsman's monogram: "N. M."

Silver, carving, engraving, gilding.

H. 28.5 cm.

Marks: Petersburg; master: "N. M."

Inv. No. PDMP 78-dm

Inscription on the stern of the ship: "Za: Fl: Ro: 1697," and "Ola: Su: Uka
C: PB: KU: 1754: May 24" ("Founding of the Russian Fleet: 1697" and
"Olanets Shipworks Order St. Petersburg Order Book: May 24,
1754").

8

TWO GOBLETS

1698–1700.

Stockholm, Sweden.

Silver, gilding, filigree, small silver balls soldered to filigree, garnets.

H. 18.5 cm.

Inv. No. PDMP 18 and 19-dm

With a lid, on three ball-legs; cup and lid decorated
with filigree and garnets.
Among Peter I's personal effects.

— 9 —

CHEST

1700s.

Tula, Russia.

Steel, bronze.

H. 27 cm.

Inv. No. PDMP 2-mt

Adorned with an imprinted monogram of Peter the First and sculptural masks of soldiers in tricorne hats; at the summit of the lid is a crown. According to legend, this chest was presented to the Emperor Peter the First by the Tula craftsmen.

Anna Ioannovna

❦

Anna Ioannovna (1693–1740). The niece of Peter I and daughter of the Tsar Ioann Alexeevich and his first wife, Praskovia Saltykova. Acceded to the throne after the death of her nephew, Emperor Peter II. Empress from 1730.

— 10 —

PORTRAIT OF THE EMPRESS
ANNA IOANNOVNA

Mid-18th century.

Unknown Russian artist.

Oil on canvas.

79.5 × 62.5 cm.

Inv. No. PDMP 1023-zh.

— 11 —

AN AWARD LADLE
PRESENTED TO THE DON ATAMAN

Moscow (?)

Silver, gilding, embossing, chasing, carving.

H. 9.6 cm.; L. 28 cm.

Inv. No. PDMP 232-dm.

Anna Ioannovna is depicted on the ladle handle, its nose adorned by a two-headed eagle; on the side of the ladle is the formal presentation inscription: "TO THE ATAMAN SEMYON SAVELEV, SON OF REBRIK, FOR HIS MANY AND TRUE SERVICES, APRIL, 1736. BY THE GRACE OF GOD WE, ANNA, EMPRESS AND SOVEREIGN OF ALL RUSSIA, PRESENTED THIS LADLE OF THE WINTER VILLAGE OF THE DON COSSACK ARMY."

— 12 —

AWARD CUP

1736.

Revel [Tallinn].

Walentin Adrian, master (1714–1753).

Silver, gilding, engraving.

H. 18.7 cm.; L. 12.6 cm.

Marks: mark of the city of Revel; masters: "VA" and "R."

Inv. No. PDMP 727-dm.

Along the edge of the lip is the inscription: "On the 20th day of June 1736, for the capture of and attack on Ozov, named by personal decree of Her Imperial Majesty the Empress Anna Ioannovna, to the fleet lieutenant Gur Ignatiev, son of Kostamarov, a sum of money was awarded, with which was made this glass."

Gur Kostamarov served in the Russian fleet from 1717 to 1761. In 1736 he participated in the taking of Azov and for this was rewarded by the Empress Anna Ioannovna.

— 13 —

"UNICORN" GOBLET

1650–1660.

Frankfurt (?), Germany.

Ivory, carving, silver, gilding, garnets.

H. 24.3 cm.

Inv. No. PDMP 1021-dm

With a carved image of a unicorn on the cup of the goblet and a sculptural one on the lid.

— 14 —

MUG WITH LID

1650–1689.

Munich (?), Germany.

Craftsman's monogram: "T. G."

Silver, gilding, embossing, carving.

H. 26 cm.

Inv. No. PDMP 221-dm

With plant ornaments and pictures of a warrior, an old man, and Minerva on medallions on the body of the mug and of a warrior in a boat on the lid.

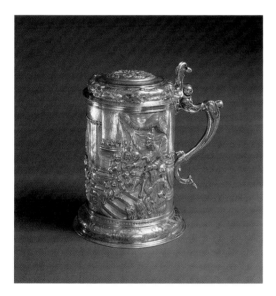

— 15 —

MUG WITH LID

1160–1680.

Koenigsberg, Germany.

Lorenz Hoffman (1631–c. 1684).

Silver, gilding, embossing, carving, engraving.

H. 24.5 cm.

Mark: "HLM."

Inv. No. PDMP 220-dm

On the body of the mug a bas-relief entitled "Solomon and the Queen of Sheba;" on the lid, "Love Conquering Time."

— 16 —

HORN WITH PORTRAIT OF ANNA IOANNOVNA

1825–1850.

Russia.

Ivory, carving.

H. 60 cm.

Inv. No. PDMP 25-bk

The horn is decorated over its entire surface with a carved relief of a hunt scene, the attributes of the Tsar's power, and plant ornament. In the central part of the horn, in oval medallions, are carved portraits of Peter the First and Anna Ioannovna. A similar horn was used during hunts.

Elizabeth Petrovna

⁓ • ⁓

Elizabeth Petrovna (1709–1761), the daughter of Emperor Peter I (the Great) and his wife, Empress Catherine I. Empress from 1741.

⁓ 17 ⁓

PORTRAIT OF
THE EMPRESS ELIZABETH PETROVNA
1760.

Carl Van Loo (1705–1765)

Oil on canvas.

146 × 113.5 cm.

On the right, on the base of the column,
signature and date: Van Loo 1760.

Inv. No. PDMP 858-zh.

— 18 —
TOILET MIRROR
1748–1755.

Paris, France.

Francois-Thomas Germain (1726–1761).

Silver, chasing, glass, woven silver cords, velvet.

H. 81.5 cm.

Inscription on the frame: "Fait par F. T. Germain sculpr
ORFRE DU ROY AUX GALLERIES DU LOUVRE A PARIS."

Inv. No. PDMP 81-dm

On the upper part of the frame, the national coat of arms of Russia flanked by two heads of cupids. Legend has it that the mirror was given to the Empress Elizabeth Petrovna by the French King Louis XV as a diplomatic gift.

— 19 —
TWO CANDELABRAS
1750–1751.

Petersburg, Russia.

Johann Frederik Kepping (?–1783).

Silver, chasing, carving.

H. 34.5 cm.

Marks: "IFK", "1750" (inv. No. 188) and the coat of arms of Russia.

Inv. No. PDMP 188, 189-dm.

For two candles; ornamented with rocaille (shell) ornament and grapevines.

— 20 —
CUP
1753.

Moscow.

Feodor Petrov.

Silver, embossing, carving, gilding.

H. 8.1 cm.

Marks: Moscow, with date, 1753. Master: "M F P".

Inv. No. PDMP 285-dm.

With three medallions surrounded by borders and shells.

— 21 —
CUP
1769.

Moscow.

F. Kryzhov (1710–?).

Silver, chasing, carving.

H. 7.5 cm.

Marks: Moscow, with date, 1769. Master: "FK".

Inv. No. 286-dm.

With ornament in the form of rocaille (shells), flowers and birds.

— 22 —

SNUFF BOX

1750–1756.

Chantilly, France.

Julien Berta (tax farmer).

Porcelain, multicolored painting, silver.

3.9 × 8.2 × 6.8 cm.

Marks: a beak and the mark of the tax farmer.

In the shape of a shell with painting of Japanese people
in an outdoor setting.

— 23 —

SNUFF BOX

1750–1760.

Saxony.

Feldspar, silver, engraving.

4.6 × 7.8 × 6.1 cm.

Inv. No. PDMP 536-dm

In the form of a chest with hinged lid.

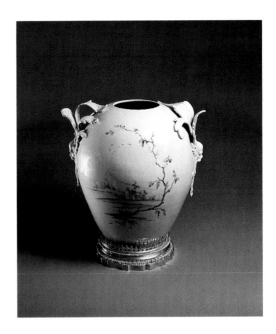

— 24 —

GOBLET

Mid-18th century.

Petersburg, Russia.

Imperial Glass Works.

Colorless glass, engraving.

H. 26 cm.

Inv. No. PDMP 1166-st

On one side, a portrait of the Empress Elizabeth Petro-vna; on the other, her monogram, "EP I" (Elizabeth Petrovna the First).

— 25 —

GOBLET

18th century.

Petersburg, Russia.

Imperial Glass Works.

Colorless glass, engraving.

H. 21 cm.

Inv. No. PDMP 2904-st

On one side, the coat of arms of the Russian Empire, two-headed eagle under a crown; on the other, the monogram "EP I".

— 26 —

VASE

1759–1760.

Petersburg, Russia.

Imperial Glass Works.

Johann Gotfried Muller (?).

Porcelain, painting in cobalt under glaze; gilded bronze attachments on the base.

H. 30 cm.

Marks: blue, under glaze: two-headed eagle under a crown; and circle with arrow.

Inv. No. PDMP 866-f

With modeled handles in the form of sculptural masks and water vegetation; on the body of the vase, landscapes.

Peter III

— • —

Peter III Feodorovich (1728–1762). Grandson of Peter I, son of the Duke Karl Friedrich Golshtein-Gottorp and the Tsarevna Anna, daughter of the Emperor Peter I (the Great). Acceded to the throne after the death of the Empress Elizabeth Petrovna. Emperor from 1761.

— 27 —

PORTRAIT OF EMPEROR PETER III

Last third of the 18th century.

Unknown Russian artist.

Oil on canvas.

56.5 × 46.5 cm.

Inv. No. PDMP 952-zh

— 28 —

DRESS UNIFORM OF PETER III

1750–1762.

Russia.

Silk reps, silk, galloon lace, metal, gilding.

H. 107 cm.

Inv. No. PDMP 380-tk.

This full-dress tunic, fashioned after the Prussian military uniform, is made of blue silk reps; the cuffs and lining are of pink silk, finished with gilded galloon lace; it closes with gilded metal buttons.

— 29 —

PETER III'S COCKED UNIFORM HAT

1750–1762.

Warsaw, Poland.

Wilhelm Neumany.

Felt, galloon lace, silk, leather.

H. 21 cm.

Marks: on the bottom, a white master's hallmark of an eagle with raised wings and the inscription: "WILHELM NEUMANY przy Ulicy Miodowey No. 492 w Warszawie".

Inv. No. PDMP 381-tk

The cocked tricorne hat matching the Prussian uniform of Peter III. Made of black felt and trimmed with gilded galloon lace.

— 30 —

PETER III'S SCARF

1750–1762.

Russia.

Silk and gilded thread.

H. 126 cm.

Inv. No. PDMP 382-tk.

The scarf from Peter III's Prussian uniform, made of gilded silk with red and light blue stripes, with double tassels on the end. Such scarfs were worn with dress uniforms as a belt or as a cross-belt for securing a sword. Legend has it that it was with this scarf that Emperor Peter III, by the order of his spouse, Catherine II, was strangled by conspirators in the Ropsha Palace.

— 31 —

FOUR FIGURES FROM THE SERIES
"TOY SOLDIERS"

c. 1745.

Meissen, Germany.

Royal Porcelain Works.

From a model by I. I. Kender (1706–1775).

Porcelain, multicolored painting over glaze, gilding.

H. 23, 22, 20, and 23 cm.

Marks: Blue marks under glaze: crossed swords.

Inv. No. PDMP 3764-3767-f.

Executed by order of the Prussian King Friedrich II as a gift to the Russian Tsarevich Peter (the future Emperor Peter III), who spent his entire childhood in Germany. Peter worshipped Friedrich II and his military system. This passion expressed itself first in playing at soldiers, and later in Peter's love for uniforms and military drills.

Catherine II (The Great)

—·—

Catherine II (The Great) (1729–1796). German princess Sophia Frederika Augusta of Anhalt-Zerbst. Her accession to the throne (after her husband, the Emperor Peter II) was by means of a coup d'etat. Empress from 1762.

— 32 —

PORTRAIT OF THE EMPRESS CATHERINE II
THE LAWGIVER IN THE CATHEDRAL OF THEMIS

Last third of the 18th century.

Unknown Russian artist.

Copy from D. Levitsky (1735–1822).

Oil on canvas.

253.5 × 176.5 cm.

Inv. No. PDMP 980-zh

— 33 —

PORTRAIT OF THE EMPRESS CATHERINE II

Nikolai Ivanovich Utkin (1780–1863).
1827.

After a portrait by V. Borovikovsky executed in 1800–1810.

Print from an etching.

64.5 × 47 cm.

Under picture on the left: Drawn by V. Borovikovsky;
on the right: engraved by Nikolai Utkin, E. I. V. Printmaker,
Member of the Academy St. Petersburg: Stockholm and Antwerp.
CATHERINE THE SECOND. To his Imperial Majesty
NICHOLAS I, His Highness the All-Russian Emperor and
Sovereign. 1827. Dedicated by the most loyal Nikolai Utkin.

Inv. No. PDMP 2302-gr.

The Empress Catherine II is shown at the age of 65
years, promenading, accompanied by her favorite Italian greyhound Zemira (Cat. No. 37), along an alley in
a Tsarskoe Selo park.

This engraving enjoyed great success. One print
was acquired by the widowed Empress Maria Feodorovna for her portrait room in the Winter Palace.

— 34 —

SNUFF BOX

1770–1777.

Paris, France.

Francois Joubert (master, 1749–1793).

Gold, multicolored translucent enamel on guilloche
ornamentation, painted.

2.5 × 8.3 × 6 cm.

Mark: "FJ" under a stylized crown

Inv. No. PDMP 751-dm

On the lid, a medallion with a depiction of a cupid with an arrow.

— 35 —

SNUFF BOX

1774–1780.

Paris, France.

Gold, multicolored enamel, painting on enamel.

Diameter: 6.1 cm.

Mark: two crossed branches under a crown.

Inv. No. PDMP 750-dm

On the cover, a painting of ruins.

— 36 —

SNUFF BOX

1780–1790.

Paris, France.

Gold, tortoiseshell, silver, ivory, painting.

Diameter: 7.9 cm.

Inv. No. PDMP 537-dm.

On the cover, a miniature on ivory: a girl with a bird.

— 37 —

FIGURE OF THE ITALIAN GREYHOUND ZEMIRA

1780s.

Imperial Porcelain Factory of Russia, Petersburg.

Model by Jacques-Dominique Rachette, 1744–1809.

Porcelain, multicolored painting over glaze, gilding.

H. 29 cm.

Inv. No. PDMP 842-f.

Two Italian Greyhound dogs, named Sir Tom Anderson and Lady Anderson, were presented to Catherine II by the English Baron Dimsdale. Among the many descendants of these dogs, an Italian greyhound by the name of Zemira was particularly loved by the Empress, who repeatedly mentioned the dog in her letters. In the park at Tsarskoe Selo, at Zemira's burial site, a stone has been preserved bearing an epitaph composed by L. P. de Segure at the request of Catherine II.

— 38 —

GOWN VERSION OF FULL-DRESS UNIFORM
OF THE FLEET OF CATHERINE II

1796.

Petersburg, Russia.

Silk reps, gold embroidery, gilded copper.

H. of bodice: 55 cm.

H. of skirt: 115 cm.

H. of "kazakin" overcoat: 205 cm.

Inv. No. PDMP 383-385-tk.

The dress consists of a bodice, a skirt, and an open outer robe of green and white silk reps decorated with gold embroidery in the form of stylized plant ornament and gilded copper buttons. Dress uniform gowns were introduced by Catherine II as a woman's version of the uniforms of the military units of which she was commander-in-chief. These women's uniforms united some distinguishing marks of military uniforms with elements of both old Russian woman's attire and European dress of the second half of the 18th century.

— 39 —

SHOES OF CATHERINE II

1750–1800.

Russia.

Silk, galloon lace, leather.

H. 10 cm.

Inv. No. PDMP 561/1,2-tk

Silk shoes on a fancy high heel, with no back, decorated over the toe with silver galloon lace. Such slippers were made without differentiation between
right and left foot, and women wearing such shoes
could walk only in very small steps. Such footwear
was intended to be worn indoors only.

— 40 —

FAN

1770–1780.

France.

Ivory, silk, sequins, carving, gilding, painted.

H. 28 cm.

Inv. No. PDMP 1628-tk

A folding fan mounted on elephant ivory with carved
gilded ornament; silk with watercolor painting and
gold. Folding fans appeared in Russia not earlier than
the early 18th century. They were brought primarily
from France, England, and Germany. This fan is of
particular interest for its "gallant scenes" with detailed
narrations of objects and costumes of the period.

— 41 —

RIDING HARNESS OF CATHERINE II'S HORSE

Mid-18th century.

Russia.

Velvet, gold embroidery, leather, metal.

H. of saddle: 59 cm.

Inv. No. PDMP 239, 239/1-7-bk

The riding harness for Catherine II's favorite horse,
named Diamond, on which Catherine travelled at the
head of her troops from Petersburg to Peterhof on the
night of June 30 [July 11th], 1762, in order to personally take part in the arrest of the overthrown Emperor
Peter III.

Paul I

—·—

Paul I (Pavel Petrovich) (1754–1801). Son of the Emperor Peter III and Catherine I (the Great). Acceded to the throne after the death of his mother. Emperor from 1796. Was strangled by conspirators in the sleeping chamber of his own palace in Petersburg (Cat. No. 49).

— 42 —

PORTRAIT OF THE EMPEROR PAUL I

Early 19th century.

Unknown Russian artist.

In the style of Jean Louis Voille, 1744–1803.

Oil on canvas.

72.5 × 51 cm.

Inv. No. PDMP 953-zh

— 43 —

PORTRAIT OF THE EMPRESS MARIA FEODOROVNA

1801.

Gerhard Kugelhen (1772–1820).

Oil on canvas.

71 × 55.5 cm.

On left, signature: G. Kugelhen. 1801.

Inv. No. PDMP 954-zh.

Maria Feodorovna (1759–1828). Wurttemberg Princess Sofia-Dorotea-Augusta-Luisa. Second wife of Paul I (Petrovich). Mother of the Emperor Alexander I.

In the portrait the Empress is shown in mourning, in the year her husband was murdered.

— 44 —

SMALL VASE

1580–1600.

Italy.

Agate, emeralds, silver, gilding, enamel.

H. 15.5 cm.

Inv. No. PDMP 1020-dm.

In the form of a shell, on a high stem, body and base decorated with emeralds and enamel.

— 45 —

VASE

Porcelain–1736–1795, China, Tsian Lun period;
Bronze–1801, Russia.

Based on a drawing by A. N. Voronikhin (1759–1814).

Porcelain, grey crackle glazing; bronze, chasing, gilding.

H. 38 cm.

Inv. No. PDMP 2495-f.

A vase in the form of a baluster, surface covered with cracks (crackle glaze); bronze fittings consist of handles in the form of winged dragons, two sculptural masks, and a square plinth.

— 46 —

SLIPPERS OF EMPEROR PAUL I

End of the 18th century.

Russia.

Brocade, thin suede, spangles, stitching.

Length: 25 cm.

Inv. No. PDMP 377-tk

Slippers of white brocade, on a low heel, decorated with spangles.

— 47 —

PURSE

1780–1800.

Russia.

Silk, satin-stitch embroidery.

H. 10.5 cm.

Inv. No. PDMP 1085-bk

Purse of white satin with shadow silk-stitch embroidery; on one side is a picture of a man fleeing from a woman shooting at him from a bow. They are dressed in antique costume. On the other side is an illustration of a flower garland, doves, and a wreath with the inscription "Love and Friendship."

The custom of embroidering purses, tobacco pouches, and pipe cases, often accompanied by sentimental inscriptions, as presents for their cavaliers, was widespread among Russian ladies and girls of the gentry in the 18th and 19th centuries.

Alexander I

— • —

Alexander I (Pavlovich) (1777–1825) was the eldest son of the Emperor Paul I and his second wife, the Empress Maria Feodorovna. Acceded to the throne after his father was murdered as the result of a court conspiracy. Emperor from 1801. Defeated Napoleon Bonaparte in the War of 1812.

— 48 —

PORTRAIT OF THE EMPEROR ALEXANDER I

1825.

George Dawe (1781–1829).

Oil on canvas.

240.5 × 152.2 cm.

On the lower right, signature and date: Geo Dawe R A pinxit SPetersburg 1825.

Inv. No. PDMP 758-zh.

— 49 —

TWIN BUSTS OF THE EMPEROR ALEXANDER I
AND THE EMPRESS ELIZABETH ALEXEEVNA

Before 1809.

France.

Unknown sculptor.

Bronze with gilding and patina.

H. 54.5 cm.

Inv. No. PDMP 860, 861-sk

Attached to the bases are gilded two-headed eagles;
one eagle's head holds an olive branch in its beak; in
the beak of the other, inclined towards its breast, is a
shield with the monogram "A and EA".

— 50 —

INKWELL ENSEMBLE OF ALEXANDER I

1800–1810.

Petersburg, Russia.

Axel Hedlund (1764–1833).

Silver, embossed.

H. 17.7 cm.

Marks: Petersburg; master: "AHL", "84", "A. Ia".

Inv. No. PDMP 310/1-4-dm

Resting on four sphinxes as legs, with three crystal
glasses for ink, sand, and quills; the figure of a swan in
the center.

— 51 —

TWO CANDLESTICKS

1800–1810.

Petersburg, Russia.

Gotthard Ferdinand Stang (1780–1821).

Silver, embossed.

H. 14 cm.

Mark: master: ""G.F.ST"

Inv. No. PDMP 73, 74-dm

In the form of figures of swans.
Matches the ink ensemble.

Note to no.s 54, 55, and 56: Personal effects of Alexander I. According to legend, this ink ensemble accompanied him during his campaign against Napoleon's troops.

— 52 —

CANDLESTICK-MIRACLE

1800–1810.

Petersburg, Russia.

Craftsman's monogram: "AHB"

Silver, chasing

H. 44 cm.

Marks: Petersburg; "84"; master: "AHB"

Inv. No. PDMP 307-dm

On a circular saucer; in the center: cup for candle surrounded by three swans; on the side, a support with a screen and a candle-snuff.

— 53 —

INCENSE BURNERS

1790–1800.

Russia.

Jasper, rhodonite, bronze.

H. 51 cm.

Inv. No.s PDMP 2416-mt; 2417-mt.

Of rhodonite and jasper, trimmed with gilded bronze; in the form of oval vases with removable lids, on a cylindrical pedestal. Square base.

— 54 —

DRESS UNIFORM OF ALEXANDER I

1813–1825.

Russia.

Broadcloth, metal.

H. 97 cm.

Inv. No. PDMP 51-tk.

This uniform of the Mounted Ranger Regiment of
the Royal Guards is of dark blue broadcloth, with silver epaulets. The collar, cuffs, and piping are from red
broadcloth, with silver stitching on the collar and
cuffs. Fastened with metal buttons. The trousers are
of dark blue broadcloth with side stripes.

— 55 —

MILITARY CAP OF ALEXANDER I

1813–1825.

Russia.

Leathern fabric, leather.

H. 14 cm.

Inv. No. PDMP 47-tk.

Military cap of black leathern fabric. The cap with a visor was introduced in Russia as part of the officer's uniform in 1811.

— 56 —

SCARF OF EMPEROR ALEXANDER I

1813–1825.

Russia.

Silk with silver threads.

H. 224 cm.

Inv. No. PDMP 48-tk.

Sash of silver silk with tassels of the same threads. A part of general's and officer's presentation uniforms. Worn around the waist and tied on the left side.

— 57 —

CARTRIDGE POUCH
OF THE EMPEROR ALEXANDER I

1813–1825.

Russia.

Leather, metal, silver thread.

H. 5.2 cm.

Inv. No. PDMP 53-tk.

Cartridge pouch of black leather with a silver strap; on the cover, a star of the order of the Holy Apostle Andrei Pervozvanny, with the motto: "For faith and loyalty." Such pouches were used for storing cartridges and were worn on a strap over the left shoulder. Part of the uniform of cavalry and mounted artillery officers.

— 58 —

JACKBOOTS OF THE EMPEROR ALEXANDER I

1813–1825.

Russia.

Leather.

H. 59 cm.

Inv. No. PDMP 54/1,2-tk.

"Hessian" military boots of black leather. Important in the design was the guard for the knee and the notch below the knee. In the Russian army, this was part of the cavalry guard regimental uniform from 1700 on.

(Photo appears on page 58.)

Nicholas I

— • —

Nicholas I (Nicholas Pavlovich) (1796–1855). Third son of the Emperor Paul I and his second wife, Maria Feodorovna. Acceded to the throne after the death of his brother Alexander I and the abdication from the throne of his brother Konstantin Pavlovich. Emperor from 1825.

— **59** —

PORTRAIT OF THE EMPEROR NICHOLAS I

1820s.

George Dawe.

Oil on Canvas.

269 × 184 cm.

Inv. No. PDMP 981-zh.

— 60 —

PORTRAIT OF THE GRAND DUCHESS
OLGA NIKOLAEVNA

1840s.

Christina Robertson (1796–1854).

Oil on canvas.

257 × 198 cm.

Inv. No. PDMP 1093-zh.

Olga Nikolaevna (1822–1892), Grand Duchess, was
the second daughter of Nicholas I and his wife
Alexandra Feodorovna. Married King Friedrich-Karl-
Alexander of Wurttemberg. The wedding ceremony
and festivities were held at Peterhof.

– 61 –

PORTRAIT OF THE GRAND DUCHESS
ALEXANDRA NIKOLAEVNA

1840s.

Christina Robertson.

Oil on canvas.

257 × 164 cm.

Inv. No. PDMP 1095-zh.

Alexandra Nikolaevna (1825–1844) was the youngest daughter of Nicholas I and his wife, Alexandra Feodorovna. Wife of Prince Friedrich of Hessen-Kassel. Died during a premature delivery along with her newborn son.

— 62 —

BUST OF THE EMPRESS
ALEXANDRA FEODOROVNA

1841.

From a 1826 model.

Petersburg, Russia.

Christian-Daniel Rauch (1777–1857).

Casting by Pyotr Karlovich Klodt (1802–1867).

Bronze with patina.

H. 68 cm.

On the back side, signature and date: "Original created by Rauch
of copper; cast by Klot 1841".

Inv. No. PDMP 616-sk

This portrait bust of Alexandra Feodorovna was
erected in the Alexandria Park of Peterhof, inside an
eight-sided iron open-work pavilion designed by the
architect A. Stackenschneider. Following the wishes
of Nicholas I, a bronze plate with the inscription:
"Joy of my life" was attached to the pedestal of the
sculpture.

— 63 —

BOX

End of 18th–early 19th century.

Germany?

Onyx, silver, gilding, painting in enamel, garnets,
almandine garnets, turquoise.

H. 7.2 cm.

Inv. No. PDMP 43-dm.

Adorned with garnets and turquoise; bottom and lid
of box of onyx.

This box was among the personal effects of the
Empress Alexandra Feodorovna. In it she kept gold
thread which she used in embroidery.

━ 64 ━
TABLE
1850–1860.

Russia.

Gilded bronze, malachite.

H. 76 cm.

Inv. No. PDMP 1704-mb.

The round malachite table top rests on a cast bronze leg decorated with figures of putti making music, garlands of flowers, and fruit.

Objects made of malachite were enormously popular in the 19th century. The craftsmen of the Peterhof Lapidary Works were considered among the most talented. They created a wide variety of objects of extraordinary beauty from this stone, the most renowned of which is the Malachite Hall of the Hermitage in Petersburg.

━ 65 ━
WRITING ENSEMBLE
1820–1825.

Petersburg, Russia.

Peterhof Lapidary Works.

Malachite, gilded bronze.

H. 33.6 cm. (ink ensemble); H. 12.5 cm. (glass);
H. 7.1 cm. (quill-cleaner).

Inv. No. PDMP 2411, 2414, 2415-mt.

The set consists of an inkwell set, a glass for quills and quill-cleaner.

The base of the inkwell set is rectangular, on four legs fashioned in the form of eagles' talons; with a sliding box on which there is a sandbox, inkpot, and small bell, all in the form of little vases.

━ 66 ━
BOX
1820–1825.

Petersburg, Russia.

Peterhof Lapidary Works.

Malachite, gilded bronze.

H. 10. 6 cm.

Inv. No. PDMP 108-mt.

Rectangular, mounted in bronze, with four legs fashioned in the form of griffins.

Part of a writing ensemble.

━ 67 ━
FOUR VASES
1820–1825.

Petersburg, Russia.

Peterhof Lapidary Works.

Malachite, gilded bronze.

H. 17.8 cm. and 30.5 cm.

Inv. No.s PDMP 107, 2435, 2412, 2413-mt.

Two rectangular and two round vases, on high legs and rectangular pedestals trimmed in gilded bronze.

Part of a writing ensemble.

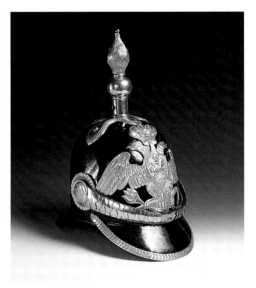

～ 68 ～

CANDELABRA

1820s.

Paris, France.

Made according to a design
by Pierre-Philippe Thomire (1751–1843).

Bronze master: Pierre-Victor Ledure (1783–after 1840).

Gilded bronze, malachite.

H. 108.5 cm.

Inv. No.s PDMP 2221, 2222-mt.

With a figure of the goddess of victory Nike, holding in raised arms a wreath with eight branches for candles; malachite plinth with bronze appliques.

    From an estate in the village of Gruzino belonging to A. Arakcheev, the Defense Minister and head of the Department of Military Affairs of the State Council. Arakcheev served under three Emperors: Paul I, Alexander I, and Nicholas I.

～ 69 ～

HELMET OF THE EMPEROR NICHOLAS I

1825–1850.

Petersburg, Russia.

Court Factory of Officer's Clothing.

Leather, metal.

H. 37 cm.

Marks: On the bottom, a paper sticker with the inscription "Court Factory of Officer's Clothing E. D. Bitner, near Anichkin Bridge, No. 10 Troitskaya St. in St. Petersburg"; over the inscription, the Russian coat of arms.

Inv. No. PDMP 235-tk.

A general's helmet of the Mounted Regiment of the Royal Guards. Black lacquer with a gilded copper coat of arms and a high, gilded, decorative summit in the form of a ball with tongues of flame.

— 70 —

UNIFORM OVERCOAT
OF THE EMPEROR NICHOLAS I

1825–1850.

Russia.

Broadcloth, metal.

H. 146 cm.

Inv. No. PDMP 57-tk.

Nicholas I's officer's overcoat, loosely tailored of grey broadcloth, with sleeves and cape and a standing collar of red broadcloth, fastened with gilded coat of arms buttons.

— 71 —

MILITARY CAP
OF THE EMPEROR NICHOLAS I

1825–1850.

Russia.

Felt, leather.

H. 12 cm.

Inv. No. PDMP 56-tk.

A standard military cap of the upper ranks of officers of all troops. White felt with red cap band and black leather visor.

Alexander II

— • —

Alexander II (Alexander Nikolaevich) (1818–1881).
Eldest son of the Emperor Nicholas I and his wife, the
Empress Alexandra Feodorovna. Acceded to the
throne after the death of his father. Emperor from
1855. Was executed according to a verdict passed by
the "Will of the People" Executive Committee.

— 72 —

PORTRAIT OF THE EMPEROR ALEXANDER II
1870–1880.
Unknown Russian artist.
Oil on canvas.
68.5 × 56 cm.
Inv. No. PDMP 1172-zh.

— 73 —

PORTRAIT OF THE EMPRESS
MARIA ALEXANDROVNA

1860.

Feodor Nikitin (?–1873)

Oil on canvas.

78.5 × 59.5 cm.

On the lower left, signature and date: F. Nikitin 1860.

Inv. No. PDMP 1339-zh.

Maria Alexandrovna (1824–1880). Daughter of the Grand Duke Louis II (Hessen) and the Princess Maximiliana-Wilhelmina-Augusta-Sofia-Maria. In 1841, married Grand Duke Alexander Nikolaevich, the future Alexander II.

— 74 —

CORONATION THRONE OF THE EMPRESS
MARIA ALEXANDROVNA

1856.

Petersburg, Russia.

Factory of the Lizere Brothers.

Linden wood, carving, gold leaf, coloring;
brocade, embroidery, applique, silver.

H. 215 cm.

Inv. No. PDMP 1719, 1720-mb.

This throne was prepared for the Andreevsky Hall of the Great Palace of the Kremlin for the coronation of Alexander II and Maria Alexandrovna in 1856. Restored in 1881 at the Moscow Schmidt factory, it was, in accordance with tradition, used again, this time in the coronation ceremony of Alexander III and Maria Feodorovna in 1882. Before 1917 the throne was in the collection at the Hall of Arms of the Moscow Kremlin.

(Currently under restoration, as seen in exhibit.)

— 75 —

BOOK: DESCRIPTION OF THE HOLY
CORONATION OF THEIR IMPERIAL
MAJESTIES THE EMPEROR ALEXANDER
THE SECOND AND THE EMPRESS
MARIA ALEXANDROVNA

1856.

Petersburg, Russia.

Printing-House of the Imperial Academy of Sciences.

Leather, brass, gold leaf; paper, chromium-plate
lithography.

92 × 70 × 6 cm.

Inv. No.s PDMP 206, 206/1-17-rk.

The book is bound in leather embossed with the imperial standards, the coats of arms of the provinces of Russia, topped with crowns, and the monogram of the Emperor Alexander II and the Empress Maria Alexandrovna under a crown and the inscription "God is With Us." On the corners of the cover and in the center of the lower cover are gilded brass fittings with Byzantine-style ornament. The clasps are made in the same fashion. Triple gold edges. Title page and chapters of the book decorated with ornamental frames and illumination, executed after the drawings of architect and artist Hippolyte Monigetti (1819–1878). In the book there are 17 chromium-plate lithographs with water coloring by artists M. A. Zichi, V. F. Timm, P. Blanchard, and others, made in Paris at the printing-house of J. R. Lemercier (1803–1887), one of the best lithographers of Europe. These lithographs reproduce fragments of scenes of the coronation festivities: the bow before the people at the Red Staircase of the Hall of Facets of the Moscow Kremlin, festive illuminations, a panorama of celebrations in the festive ancient Russian capital Moscow, and others. Coronation volumes commemorating these important formal ceremonies were traditionally issued in Russia, beginning with the accession to the throne of Anna Ioannovna (1730). The description of the coronation of the Emperor Alexander II is the biggest Russian book. The ritual of coronation in Russia was not simply a solemn and majestic custom, but also an important political act of transfer of power. From the time of Peter the Great on it was one of the most significant and solemn occasions in the life of each monarch. Representatives of the many ethnic groups of Russia traveled from all corners of the Empire to be present at the coronation of Alexander II. All of the great states of the world sent special ambassadors: the Emperor Napoleon sent Count Morny, the Austrian Emperor Franz-Josef sent Prince Esterhazy, the Queen of England sent Lord Grenville, and G. Seymour, special envoy and plenipotentiary minister, came from America.

ILLUSTRATIONS FROM THE CORONATION BOOK

— 76 —

PROCLAMATION OF THE CORONATION
ON RED SQUARE

Printing-house of Lemercier (Paris).

Lithography by J. David and J. Arnout,
based on drawings by V. F. Timm (1820–1895).

Paper, colored lithograph.

69.7 × 89.7 cm.

Inv. No. PDMP 206/5-rk.

In Russia, from the early 18th century on, it was customary to herald the day of the upcoming coronation. An equestrian detachment, including adjutant-generals, senior masters of ceremonies, heralds, kettledrummers, and trumpeters both formally announced to the public the day of the coronation and handed out announcements explaining the order of the ceremonies. The Emperor Alexander II was crowned on August 26, 1856, having made his coronation plans public in a special manifesto. Depicted here is one of the three days before the coronation, during which heralds announced and described the upcoming festivities to the people, who, gathered on Red Square near the monument to Prince Pozharsky and Minin, received sheets of paper with the proclamation to the strains of the anthem "God Keep the Tsar".

ILLUSTRATIONS FROM THE CORONATION BOOK

— 77 —

THE SUPREME DINNER TABLE
AT THE HALL OF FACETS

Printing-house of Lemercier (Paris)

Lithography by E. David,
based on drawings by V. F. Timm.

Paper, colored lithograph.

69.7 × 89.7 cm.

Inv. No. PDMP 206/13-rk.

State dinners during the days of the coronation were held in the Hall of Facets of the Kremlin Palace, and included several hundred invited guests. At Alexander II's coronation banquet the table was set with golden plates and utensils and with a porcelain service made in Sevres, with cameos and the monogram of Catherine II. Dinner was accompanied by music and song, and toasts were pronounced to the sound of trumpets and kettledrums. At table, Alexander II sat between his spouse, Maria Alexandrovna, and his mother, the widowed Empress Alexandra Feodorovna (1798–1860).

— 78 —

BAPTISMAL CHEST

1817–1818.

Petersburg, Russia.

Peterhof Lapidary Works (?) (processing of stones)

Bronze, gilding, silver, chasing, painting,
semi-precious and other stone.

14.9 × 27 × 18 cm.

Inv. No. PDMP 1024-dm.

Gilded bronze decorated with semi-precious stones;
on the inside of the lid, the head of Christ in a crown
of thorns.

    The chest was intended to hold the christening at-
tire of the heir to the throne, the Grand Duke Alexander Nikolaevich.

— 79 —

COPY OF THE CHRISTENING ATTIRE OF THE
GRAND DUKE ALEXANDER NIKOLAEVICH

1996.

St. Petersburg, Russia.

Students of Girls' Gymnasium 628.

Batiste, satin-stitch embroidery in silk, drawn-thread work.

H. 60 cm.

Inv. No. PDMP 1140, 1141-tk.

Shirt and bonnet of white batiste embroidered over
the entire surface with small flowers and finished
with double flounces. This baptismal attire, which re-
places the original christening clothing of the Grand
Duke Alexander Nikolaevich, destroyed after 1917,
was reproduced according to a watercolor portrait of
Alexander II as a child and historical analogues.

— 80 —

PAPER WEIGHT WITH PORTRAIT OF
THE GRAND DUKE ALEXANDER NIKOLAEVICH

1818–1819.

Petersburg, Russia.

Peterhof Lapidary Works (malachite).

Unknown artist (miniature on ivory).

Malachite, gold, bronze, gilding; ivory, watercolor.

H. 12.3 cm.

Inv. No. PDMP 60-dm.

A two-sided miniature with a depiction of the Grand
Duke Alexander Nikolaevich (the future Emperor of
Russia Alexander II) in infancy, on a malachite base.

— 81 —

INK SET

1875.

Petersburg, Russia.

Peterhof Lapidary Works.

M. A. Chizhov (sculptor, 1838–1916).

"Nikols and Plinke" Co. (silver) (Konstantin
Nikols and Vasili Plinke; in business
1809–1852).

Craftsman's monogram: "PK" (jeweler).

Silver, chasing, carving, jasper, Roman mosaic.

H. 56 cm.

Marks: Petersburg, with mark of assay "84"; coat
of arms of Russia; firm: "NP"; master: "PK";
sculptor: "MODELED BY M. CHIZHOV".

Inv. No. 48/1, 2; 1026, 1026/1, 2-dm.

In the form of a monument of Catherine II, who is shown sitting in an armchair with a plan of the Peterhof Lapidary Works; the glasses for quills are decorated with bas-reliefs depicting putti manufacturing the ink set. On the front of the pedestal, a mosaic image of the Peterhof Lapidary Works and the inscription: "FOUNDED 1775 REBUILT 1875."

The Peterhof Lapidary Works was founded by Peter I for the processing of semi-precious and other minerals. In 1775,

by order of Catherine II, a stone edifice was built to replace the original wooden one. For its centennial anniversary, the factory received yet another building and new technical equipment.

On July 26th, 1875, on the day of the factory's dedication, this ink set was presented to the Emperor Alexander II and exhibited in the Great Palace at Peterhof.

Alexander III

— • —

Alexander III (Alexander Alexandrovich) (1845–1894).
Second son of the Emperor Alexander II and his wife,
the Empress Maria Alexandrovna. Emperor from 1881.
Acceded to the throne after the murder of his father,
Emperor Alexander II, by members of the "Will of the
People" Committee.

— 82 —

PORTRAIT OF THE EMPEROR ALEXANDER III

1889.

Pyotr Petrovich Zabolotsky (1842—not earlier than 1916).

Oil on canvas.

172 × 110 cm.

On the lower right, signature and date: P. Zabolotsky 1889.

Inv. No. PDMP 1335-zh.

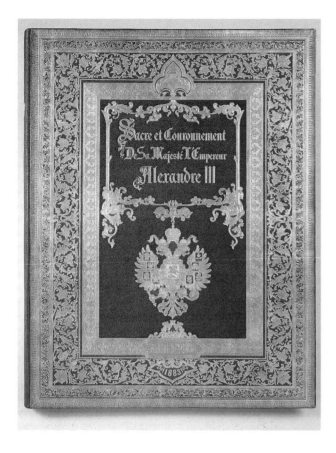

— 83 —

BOOK: DESCRIPTION OF THE HOLY CORONATION
OF THEIR IMPERIAL HIGHNESSES THE EMPEROR
OF ALL RUSSIA ALEXANDER III AND
THE EMPRESS MARIA FEODOROVNA

1883.

Petersburg, Russia.

Printing-House of the Expedition
for the Production of State Papers.

Paper, print, leather, lithographs.

67.5 × 53.5 cm.

Inv. No. PDMP 205-rk.

The leather cover of this coronation album is decorated with gilded imprints in the form of decorative frames of stylized floral ornament and two-headed Russian coats of arms in the center and, along the spine of the book, with gilded imprints of imperial regalia: crowns, scepters, and orbs. As in the coronation albums of previous monarchs, the entire sequence of coronation festivities and rituals is described here in detail; from the coronation of the Emperor at the Kremlin's Uspensky Cathedral to the Emperor's ceremonial review of the troops and his departure to Petersburg. The book is splendidly illustrated with lithographs, drawings, and brightly colored illuminations. Well-known Russian artists K. Makovsky, I. Kramskoy, V. Vereshchagin, V. Surikov, and others took part in the book's decoration.

ILLUSTRATION FROM THE BOOK

— 84 —

EMPEROR ALEXANDER III PLACES
SMALL CROWN ON THE HEAD
OF THE EMPRESS MARIA FEODOROVNA

1882.

Petersburg, Russia.

Cartographic establishment of A. Ilyin.

After an original by I. N. Kramsky (1837–1887).

Paper, colored lithography.

66 × 51 cm.

Illustration of the scene of Empress Maria Feodorovna's coronation. From the time of Peter I, the first Russian tsar to hold the title of Emperor, at the coronation the future monarch placed the crown, brought to him by the metropolitan, on himself, as an inheritance due him by birth, with the church only blessing this act of coronation. The Empress would then approach the Emperor, who was sitting on the throne. The Tsar took the crown from his head, touched the head of the Empress, and then placed on her the small crown, the mantle, and the chain of the Order of Andrei Pervozvanny.

~ 85 ~

CROUTON BOX

1882.

Moscow.

Andrei Postnikov (active during 1870–1898).

Silver, filigree, small silver balls soldered to filigree, gilding.

29.8 × 20.7 cm.

Marks: Moscow, with mark of assay "91"; master: "A. Postnikov", "A. K / 1882".

Inv. No. PDMP 25-dm.

Stylized plant ornament with filigree and small silver balls soldered to filigree; in the center, the imperial crown.

~ 86 ~

TRAY

1880s.

Moscow (?).

A. Postnikov (?).

Silver, filigree, small silver balls soldered to filigree, gilding.

34.3 × 22.6 cm.

Inv. No. PDMP 26-dm

With filigree with small silver balls soldered to filigree, stylized plant pattern and applied filigree flowers.

— 87 —

PAPER WEIGHT

1880s.

Petersburg, Russia.

Carl Fabergé (1846–1920).

Lapis lazuli, silver, chasing, carving.

22.8 × 17.9 × 9.4 cm.

Inv. No. PDMP 58-dm.

In the form of a two-tiered lapis base on which lie two silver figures of lizards.
Belonged to Maria Feodorovna, wife of Alexander III.

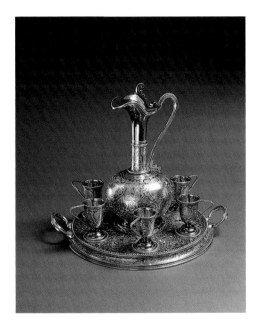

VODKA SET

1889.

Moscow, Russia.

Feodor Yartsev (active during 1881–1896).

Silver, niello, carving, gilding.

Pitcher: H. 23.3 cm.; tray: d. 25.9 cm.; cup: 6 cm.

Marks: Moscow; with mark of assay "84";
master: "FYa", "A. R/1889".

Inv. No. PDMP 654, 673-679-dm

Set consists of an Eastern-style pitcher for vodka, a round tray, and six mug cups; all items decorated with black enamel.

— 89 —

LADLE

1880–1887.

Moscow, Russia.

The Sazikov Co. (1793–1887).

Silver, gilding, filigree, multicolored enamel.

H. 13.8 cm.

Marks: "SAZIKOV", "84".

Inv. No. PDMP 776-dm

The entire outer surface and handle are decorated in multicolored enamel over filigree designs.

~ 90 ~

SALT CELLAR

1891.

Moscow, Russia.

Ivan Saltykov (active 1884–after 1900).

Silver, multicolored
cloisonne-style enamel, filigree.

H. 7.7 cm.

Marks: Moscow; "84"; master: "IS", "R. V/1891"

Inv. No. PDMP 493-dm.

In the form of an armchair-trunk, decorated with multicolored enamel.

~ 91 ~

SALT CELLAR

1890–1894.

Moscow, Russia.

Semyon Kazakov
(active 1889–after 1908).

Silver, gilding, engraving,
enamel relief.

H. 14.7 cm.

Marks: "SK", "84".

Inv. No. PDMP 358-dm.

In the form of a Russian-style well on four ball-legs.

~ 92 ~

SALT CELLAR

1896–1908.

Moscow, Russia.

Mikhail Zorin.

Silver, gilding, multicolored enamel
on filigree.

H. 5.4 cm.

Marks: "MZ", "84"; engraved: "1866 2/XI 1911".

Inv. No. PDMP 744-dm.

In the shape of a ladle with a vegetation-inspired motif in multicolored enamel.

— 93 —

VASE

1890–1894.

Copenhagen, Denmark.

Royal Porcelain Works.

Christian Groth (1863–1904), jeweler.

Porcelain, painting under glaze, silver, carving.

H. 18.5 cm.

Marks: on the porcelain: crown and three waves; *marks on the silver:* City
of Copenhagen, "925", "GS".

Inv. No. PDMP 1111-dm.

On the body of the vase, a depiction of Viking drakar boats; neck encrusted in silver applique.

Maria Feodorovna, wife of Alexander III, a Danish princess, brought a collection of porcelain of Copenhagen manufacture with her to Russia. She installed part of this collection in her study in the Cottage Palace at Peterhof.

❖ 94 ❖

PORTRAIT OF THE EMPRESS
MARIA FEODOROVNA

1883.

Pyotr Petrovich Zabolotsky

Oil on canvas.

169 × 107 cm.

On the lower right, signature and date: by P. Zabolotsky 1883.

Inv. No. PDMP 1336-zh.

Maria Feodorovna (1847–1928). Daughter of Danish
King Christian IX, Princess Maria-Sofia-Frederika-
Dagmara. In 1866 married Grand Duke Alexander
Alexandrovich, the future Emperor Alexander III.

Nicholas II

—•—

Nicholas II (Nicholas Alexandrovich) (1868–1918).
Eldest son of the Emperor Alexander III and the Empress Maria Feodorovna. Emperor from 1894. The last
Russian Emperor. In 1917, he signed an act of abdication from the throne; he was executed by firing squad
in 1918.

— 95 —

PORTRAIT OF THE EMPEROR NICHOLAS II

1900–1915.

Shilder, Nicholas (1828–1919).

Oil on canvas.

250 × 145 cm.

Bottom left: signature: N. Shilder.

Inv. No. PDMP 1334-zh.

~ 96 ~

BUST OF THE EMPRESS
ALEXANDRA FEODOROVNA,
WIFE OF THE EMPEROR NICHOLAS II

1896–1900.

Paris, France.

Ceramic Workshop of Joseph-Theodore Deck (1823–1891).

Ceramist: Lachenal Edmond (1855–?).

After an original by M. M. Antokolsky (1843–?).

Ceramic, colored glaze.

H. 64 cm.

Black inscription under glaze: ANTOCOLSKY Steur,
LACHENAL Ceramiste

Inv. No. PDMP 6893-f

In 1896 M. M. Antokolsky created a pair of marble busts of the Emperor Nicholas II and his wife, the Empress Alexandra Feodorovna.

~ 97 ~

CORONATION THRONE
OF THE EMPEROR NICHOLAS II

1896.

Moscow, Russia.

A. Schmidt Factory.

Birch, carving, gilding, bronze, silver, brocade, stitching.

H. 182 cm.

On seat frame bar, stamp: "Court fact. A. Schmidt. Moscow.";
two-headed eagles on either side.

Inv. No. PDMP 993-mb.

This coronation chair was made at the factory of A. Schmidt, purveyor to the Imperial Court, according to drawings by the official Custodian of the Armory, A. E. Komarovsky. The throne was used for the solemn coronation ceremony in 1896 and was located in the Andreevsky Hall of the Great Kremlin Palace.

— 98 —

GOBLETS AND WINE GLASSES

1912.

Petersburg, Russia.

Imperial Glass Factory.

Colorless glass, etching, engraving, monochrome painting, gilding.

H. 21.2, 20.8, 15.7, 13.6 cm.

Inv. No. PDMP 2916, 1203, 2912, 2917-st.

On one goblet, an engraved mark: N II 1912, under a crown.

With a depiction of the monogram "NA II" under a crown of the Emperor Nicholas II and a two-headed eagle under a crown with an orb and a scepter in its claws. This set of gift goblets was produced for the celebration of the tricentennial anniversary of the Imperial House of Romanovs.

~ 99 ~

OFFICER'S CIRCASSIAN UNIFORM COAT
OF HIS IMPERIAL MAJESTY'S PERSONAL CONVOY

1900–1910.

Petersburg, Russia.

Tailor to His Majesty's Personal E. V. Convoy,
Platon Monastirsky.

Broadcloth, velvet, galloon lace, metal,
gold and silver thread stitching.

H. 137 cm.

Inv. No. PDMP 684-tk.

This Circassian winter dress uniform with *aide-de-camp* colonel's epaulettes belonged to the Emperor Nicholas II. Wide trousers of blue broadcloth with a stripe and white linen shirt with galloon lace.

His Majesty's Personal Convoy was formed of Caucasian mountain men under Nicholas I in 1828. During the reign of Nicholas II, it consisted exclusively of Kuban and Tersk Cossacks. Peculiarities of the uniforms of these troops influenced the attire of the convoy as well. They wore papakhi (fur hats) and Circassian coats with red (dress) and blue cartridge pockets on the chest, wide trousers with a stripe, and high boots. The Personal Convoy served as personal guards for the Emperor and was particularly favored by the Tsar's family. Nicholas II, from 1894 to 1917, was patron of the Convoy; the Heir to the Throne was listed in the ranks of this detachment from the day of his birth.

— 100 —

DRESS OF THE EMPRESS
ALEXANDRA FEODOROVNA

1900–1910.

Russia.

Batiste, silk, lace, embroidery.

H. 180 cm.

Inv. No. PDMP 399-tk.

A morning gown of the Empress Alexandra Feodorovna, made of white batiste finished with Russian-
style stitched inserts, needlepoint embroidery, and
lace; with short sleeves, cut out at the waist, with a
short train.

— 101 —

PARASOL

1900–1910.

France.

Silk, gauze, lace, wood, porcelain, metal.

H. 106 cm.

Marks: on the metal rim, the inscription "DOUBLE".

Inv. No. PDMP 613-tk

Sun parasol of white coupled lace, with a porcelain
handle.

~ 102 ~

FAN

1900–1910.

France.

Mother-of-pearl, lace, engraving, foil.

H. 24 cm.

Inv. No. PDMP 562-bk

Fan on a mother-of-pearl frame, with carved gilded ornament; made of white handmade Brussels lace.

The Marriage Cup

(See page 105)

FABERGÉ

—•—

Peter Karl FABERGÉ (1846–1920), proprietor of a jewelry firm founded in 1842 by his father, in Petersburg. In 1864 Peter Karl Fabergé entered his father's firm, and in 1882 participated in the All-Russian Art Exhibition in Moscow and received a gold medal. In 1885 he was appointed purveyor to the Imperial Court, and created his first Easter egg on commission from the Emperor Alexander III.

In 1887, a Moscow branch of the firm opened. In 1897 Fabergé participated in the Northern Exhibition in Stockholm and received the honor of being named court jeweler to the King of Sweden and Norway.

Branches of the firm opened in Odessa in 1900, in London in 1903, and in Kiev in 1905.

In 1908 the firm began selling its work beyond the borders of Europe: in Asia, India, Siam, and China.

The finest masters of the Fabergé firm were: Mikhail Perchin, Isaac Rappoport, Andres Nevalainen, and Hjalmar Armfelt; Ivan Britzin began his career as a student in the firm.

—•—

— 103 —

TABLE CLOCK OF NICHOLAS II

1894–1896.

Petersburg, Russia.

Fabergé.

Mikhail Perchin (1860–1903).

Marble, silver, chasing, enamel.

H. 17.5 cm.

Marks: Petersburg, with mark of assay "88", "M. P".

Inv. No. PDMP 501-dm.

Dark red marble, with applied silver decoration in the form of arabesques and garlands of laurels and ribbons.

Before 1917 the clock was the personal property of Nicholas II and was kept in the Winter Palace, in the Emperor's office, on his desk.

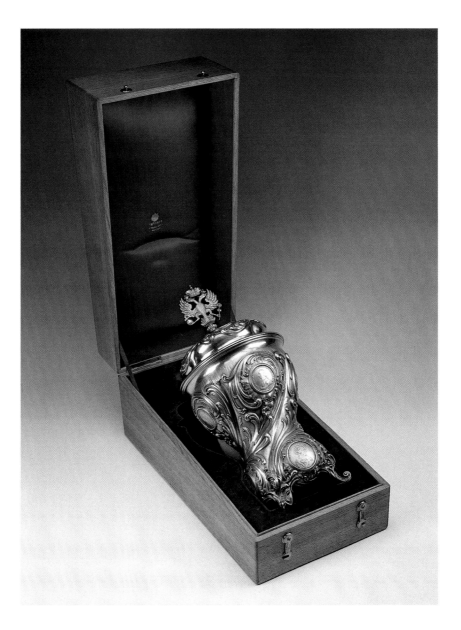

— 104 —

TROPHY CUP

1898.

Petersburg, Russia.

Fabergé.

Isaac Rappoport (1864–1916).

Cup: silver, chasing, engraving, gilding;
Case: oak, velvet, silk, brass.

H. cup: 39.7 cm.; case: 46.2 × 23.5 × 19.8 cm.

Marks: cup: "FABERGE" with a two-headed eagle, "88", "IR";
case: inside, a gold impression of the hallmark of the Fabergé firm
as purveyor to the Court, with a two-headed eagle and the
inscription: "St. Petersburg Moscow".

Inv. No. PDMP 656, 656/1-dm.

Executed in the style of 18th-century Baroque
tankard cups, with a lid crowned by a two-headed eagle; mounted on the cup and lid are coins and com-
memorative medals from the reigns of Emperors
from Peter I to Nicholas II. On the lid of the case is a
plate with the inscription: "Neva Yacht Club, the
Lord Emperor's Prize; Sail Race of the 22nd of July,
1898, at Peterhof, Yachts Perkun, Counts F. G. and
E. F. Berg".

The 1898 prize was the first prize established by
Nicholas I as a yearly prize for the Peterhof races. The
festive opening of the of the Neva Yacht Club of Peterhof Port took place on May 30th, 1898, on the day
commemorating Peter I. This first prize was won by
the Counts Berg.

— 105 —

ASHTRAY

1890–1896.

Petersburg, Russia.

Fabergé.

I. Rappoport.

Cast silver, chasing.

H. 4.2 cm.

Marks: "FABERGÉ", "I. R", "88", with the coat of arms of Petersburg.

Inv. No. PDMP 333-dm.

In the form of a seated monkey.

— 106 —

FRAME WITH PHOTOGRAPHS
OF THE TSAREVICH ALEXEI

1907–1908.

Petersburg, Russia.

Fabergé.

Hjalmar Armfelt.

Silver, gilding, enamel on a guilloche background.

H. 10.4 cm.

Marks: "FABERGE", "IaA", "88".

Inv. No. PDMP 191-dm.

Two-sided, covered in enamel—white on one side, blue on the other; with two photographs of the Tsarevich Alexei: on one side in a sailor suit and wide-brimmed hat, on the other, in the uniform of a sailor of the yacht "Standard."

― 107 ―

WINE CUPS FOR TWO

1887–1896.

Moscow, Russia.

Fabergé.

Silver, chasing, gilding.

H. 9.7 and 9.5 cm.

Marks: Moscow, with mark of assay "84", "K. F".

Inv. No.s PDMP 661, 662-dm.

In the shape of seated male and female bears.

― 108 ―

SMALL WINE CUP

1896–1903.

Petersburg, Russia.

Fabergé.

Andres Nevalainen (1858–1933).

Silver, chasing, gilding, translucent enamel
on a guilloche background.

H. 3.7 cm.

Marks: " K. FABERGE", "A. N", "88".

Inv. No. PDMP 335-dm.

In the form of a cup on three ball-legs; exterior surface
covered in white enamel.

― 109 ―

BLANK SEAL

1908–1917.

Petersburg, Russia.

Ivan Britzin.

Silver, colored gold, translucent enamel, jade, chalcedony.

H. 6.7 cm.

Marks: "I. B", "56", "84".

Inv. No. PDMP 781-dm.

Platform of the seal made of chalcedony, handle
made of jade; with silver mounting, covered in lilac
enamel.

— 110 —

BELL

1908–1917.

Petersburg, Russia.

Fabergé.

Silver, chasing, glass.

H. 7 cm.

Marks: "FABERGÉ", "88".

Inv. No. PDMP 663-dm.

In the form of a cat washing itself.

— 111 —

VASE IN A CASE

1908–1917.

Moscow, Russia.

Fabergé.

Silver, chasing, cut crystal.

H. 20.4 cm.; case: 23.7 × 32.3 × 32.3 cm.

Marks: "K. FABERGE" with coat of arms of Russia, "88".

Inv. No. PDMP 672, 672/1-dm.

Consists of two parts: a flat, round crystal vase and a silver leg in the form of three swans; in an oak case. (Case not shown).

— 112 —

BUCKLE

1903–1908.

Petersburg, Russia.

Ivan Britzin (1870–1952).

Silver, gold, translucentenamel, rubies, rose-cut diamonds.

7.3 × 5.5 cm.

Inv. No. PDMP 541-dm.

Oval in shape, decorated with white enamel and two rubies surrounded by rose-cut diamonds.

— 113 —

CLOCK-FRAME

1908–1917.

Petersburg, Russia.

Ivan Britzin.

Silver, gilding, translucent enamel.

H. 14.7 cm.

Marks: "BRITZIN", "I. B.", "88".

Inv. No. PDMP 539-dm.

In the form of a tabletop frame, in which a round clock with the signature "BRITZIN" is mounted. The rest of the frame is covered in white and blue enamel.

— 114 —

BROOCH

1903–1913.

Petersburg, Russia.

"F. Butz Co." (1849–1912).

Craftsman's monogram: "W. Z."

Gold, diamonds, sapphires, rubies.

L. 7.3 cm.

Marks: "WZ", "56"; on the case: "F. BUTTS St. PETERSBURG", with the coat of arms of Russia.

Inv. No. PDMP 1019, 1019/1-dm.

In the form of a branch with red (rubies) and blue (sapphires) berries; leaves adorned with diamonds.

— 115 —

SNUFF BOX

1909–1914.

St. Petersburg, Russia.

Henrik Wigström.

H. 2.5; oval: 7.3 × 3.9.

Oval, all its outer surfaces are decorated with polychrome views of Peterhof: view of The Great Cascade and the Palace from the bridge—on the cover, the same view from the scoop—on the bottom, and on its lateral sides are the views of Marly and Monplaisir, and two views of the lower balustrade.

Presented to the Palaces May 31, 1998 by the Rio Suite Hotel & Casino.

Forbes and Fabergé

~ • ~

Every collection begins with a first purchase that sparks the desire for more. For Malcolm S. Forbes, Sr. it was a cigarette case by Peter Carl Fabergé purchased as a Christmas present for his wife in 1960. The handsome gold case decorated with a diamond-set Imperial eagle, so delighted its recipient that the following Easter, Malcolm surprised his wife with a miniature Fabergé egg enameled white with a red cross. These two initial purchases led in 1965 to the collection's first major acquisition, the Duchess of Marlborough Egg commissioned by the Duchess of Marlborough, née Consuelo Vanderbilt, in 1902. Malcolm Forbes' enthusiastic bidding for this magnificent pink-enameled Fabergé egg-clock caught the attention of the underbidder, Alexander Schaffer, proprietor of New York's prestigious A La Vieille Russie, who invited the eager collector back to his shop to examine the contents of its safe. When the visit concluded, the Imperial Renaissance and Orange Tree Easter eggs had joined the Forbes Fabergé treasury. Over the next three decades, the collection has grown to approximately 400 *objets d'art* making it one of the world's largest, seconded only by that of the Queen of England. The collection's twelve Imperial Easter eggs, including the Imperial Chanticleer Egg purchased in 1966, is, however, the world's largest repository of these famed treasures. Visitors may view the Fabergé collection as well as those of toy soldiers, toy boats, inscribed trophies, and rotating selections from the Forbes autograph, painting, and photograph collections at The FORBES Magazine Galleries. Located on the ground level of the magazine's corporate headquarters at 62 Fifth Avenue, New York, New York, the Galleries are open free to the public Tuesday through Saturday from 10:00 A.M. to 4:00 P.M.

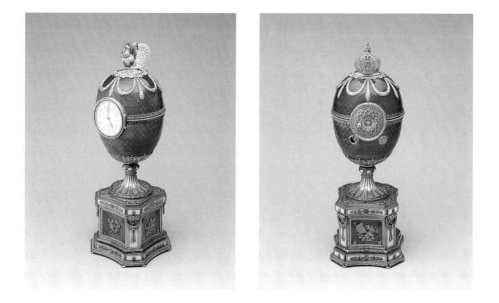

1. IMPERIAL CHANTICLEER EGG

Two-color gold, enamel, diamonds, pearls, crystal.
Original silver key.

H: 12-5/8 inches; 32 cm. open.

Marks: FABERGÉ, initials of workmaster Michael Perchin,
initials of assay-master Jakov Ljapunov,
assay mark of St. Petersburg 1896–1908, 56 (*zolotnik*)

Fabergé elevated the clock from household accessory to art form with the design of the *Imperial Chanticleer Egg.* Presented by Tsar Alexander III to Tsarina Marie Feodorovna on Easter 1903, the monumental egg in the French neo-classical style is, after the *Uspensky Cathedral Egg* of 1904, the largest Fabergé Easter egg known today. Enameled a dazzling blue over a *guillochéd* zigzag pattern, the egg is joined by a fluted gold shaft to a shaped octagonal base. The pedestal is set with four large blue *guilloché* enamel panels applied with symbols of the Arts and Sciences in two-color gold, a reference to the Tsarina's patronage of the arts. At the back of the egg is a pierced grille and two swiveling rosettes which hide the winding mechanism for which the original silver key still exists.

The clock face is covered by a rock crystal bezel bordered by seed pearls. Intricately pierced gold hands mark time by pointing to painted blue enamel numerals further embellished by green enamel foliate borders. When the hour strikes, the surprise concealed beneath a pierced grille atop the egg, is a gold chanticleer. Enameled yellow, blue and green and set with rose-cut diamonds, the bird rises automatically and bobs its head, flaps its wings and opens and closes its beak to crow the hour. Complex mechanisms in the interior of the egg control the clock and proud cockerel.

Provenance: Presented by Tsar Nicholas II to his mother, Dowager Empress Marie Feodorovna, Easter 1903; Hammer Galleries, New York; Maurice Sandoz, Switzerland; A La Vieille Russie, Inc., New York; Lansdell K. Christie, Long Island, New York.

(Photo appears on page 8.)

Credit: The FORBES Magazine Collection, New York.

2. MECKLENBURG PRESENTATION CIGARETTE CASE

Gold, sapphire

L: 3 1/2 inches; 8.9 cm.

Marks: Initials of workmaster August Wilhelm Holmström, assay mark of St. Petersburg before 1896

A gold cigarette case with a cabochon sapphire push piece presented by Grand Duke Friedrich of Mecklenburg to his aide-de-camp Alexander Maximovich Reutern. The interior, inscribed sentiment reads: En souvenir/des journées passées/ensemble à Peterhof/et en camp, Juillet 1894/Friedrich (In remembrance of days spent at Peterhof and at camp, July 1894).

Grand Duke Friedrich Franz III, Grossherzog von Mecklenburg-Schwerin (1851–1897) was the brother of Marie Pavlovna, wife of Tsar Alexander III's brother Grand Duke Vladimir. His aide-de-camp, Alexander Maximovich Reutern, was a colonel in the Preobrazhenski Guards Regiment in the 1880's and usually took part in summer maneuvers camps at Krasnoe Selo and Peterhof.

Provenance: Presented by Grand Duke Friedrich of Mecklenburg to Alexander Maximovich Reutern, 1894; Baron and Baroness Max de Reutern, Rome; Alexis P. Teissier, New York.

Credit: The FORBES Magazine Collection, New York.

A La Vieille Russie and Fabergé

Founded in Kiev in 1851, A La Vieille Russie, located at 781 Fifth Avenue in New York City, continues its tradition of dealing in fine art and antique jewelry. A La Vieille Russie moved to Paris at the time of the Russian Revolution, and to New York as World War II approached. There, in the 1930s, Alexander and Ray Schaffer introduced the works of Russian Court Jeweler Carl Fabergé to the United States, and helped form some of the world's finest Fabergé collections. Fabergé himself was a client back in Kiev, and today A La Vieille Russie is recognized as an international expert on his works. Still a multigenerational family business, the firm also deals in fine antique jewelry from throughout Europe and America, gold snuffboxes, Russian decorative arts including silver, porcelain and enamel, as well as Russian paintings and icons.

1. SNUFFBOX
1896–1908.

St. Petersburg.

Oval gold, pink, and sepia guilloché enamel snuffbox, the cover depicting St. Petersburg's fortress of Saints Peter and Paul, where Nicholas II and family members have recently been interred, and the bottom and sides painted with scenes along the River Neva. By Fabergé, workmaster Michael Perchin. Length: 2-7/8 inches; Height: 1-1/8 inches.

Credit: Lent by courtesy of A La Vieille Russie, New York.

2. BONBONNIÈRE
1903–1908.

St. Petersburg.

Circular gold and enamel bonbonnière, depicting in sepia and pink guilloché enamel landmark statues of St. Petersburg, the lid with Falconet's Peter the Great, the base with Catherine the Great. By Fabergé, workmaster Henrik Wigström. Diameter: 2-1/8 inches.

Credit: Lent by courtesy of A La Vieille Russie, New York.

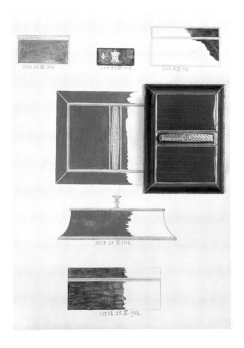

3. TABLE BOX

1908–1917.

St. Petersburg.

Large gilded silver and red guilloché enamel table box, with handle and two lidded compartments. By Fabergé, workmaster Henrik Wigström. Length: 5-5/8 inches; Width: 4-1/4 inches. With framed actual size Wigström design for the piece: The box appears in Wigström's design books, dated 12 October 1912, and was sold in Fabergé's London branch in 1912 for £60.

Credit: Lent by courtesy of A La Vieille Russie, New York.

4. MARRIAGE CUP

circa 1890.

St. Petersburg.

Gold double marriage cup, based on the Gothic tradition, each bowl a geometric pattern of four colors of textured gold. By Fabergé, workmaster Michael Perchin. Total height: 3-5/8 inches.

(Photo appears on page 94.)

Credit: Lent by courtesy of A La Vieille Russie, New York.

5. CARP

circa 1900.

St. Petersburg.

Large carved obsidian carp, with moonstone and yellow enamel eyes. By Fabergé. Length: 6-1/2 inches.

Credit: Lent by courtesy of A La Vieille Russie, New York.

6. SNUFF BOX

circa 1900.

St. Petersburg.

Oval gold and blue guilloché enamel Imperial presentation snuffbox, the cover with diamond-set crowned cypher of Tsar Nicholas II, with red guilloché enamel and diamond border. By Karl Hahn, court jeweler. Length: 3-1/2 inches.

Credit: Lent by courtesy of A La Vieille Russie, New York.

7. SCARAB-FORM CUP

circa 1900.

St. Petersburg.

Gold-mounted carved nephrite scarab-form cup, set with diamonds and cabochon ruby eyes, and with red and white enamel border. By Fabergé, workmaster Michael Perchin. Length: 3-13/16 inches; Height: 15/16 inches.

Credit: Lent by courtesy of A La Vieille Russie, New York.

8. BONBONNIÈRE

1908–1917.

St. Petersburg.

Circular nephrite bonbonnière, mounted in gold, the reeded white enamel rim with ruby-set cross ties. By Fabergé, workmaster Henrik Wigström. Diameter: 1-5/8 inches; Height: 13/16 inches.

Credit: Lent by courtesy of A La Vieille Russie, New York.

9. CLOAK CLASPS

circa 1900.

St. Petersburg.

Pair gold, enamel, green beryl, and pink amethyst cloak clasps. Length, each: 3 inches; Together: length 5-1/2 × 2-1/4 inches.

Credit: Lent by courtesy of A La Vieille Russie, New York.

10. MATCH HOLDER AND STRIKER

circa 1900.

St. Petersburg.

Silver-mounted sandstone match holder and striker, the feet inscribed Tsarkoe Peterhof, M. Troubeszkoy, N. Goudovitch. By Fabergé. Height: 3-5/8 inches.

Credit: Lent by courtesy of Dr. Edwin I. Radlauer, New York.

CHAPEL OF PETERHOF

— 116 —

GOSPELS

1829 (printed); 1834 (setting).

Petersburg, Russia.

Craftsman's monogram: "P. U." (silver).

Imperial Porcelain Factory.

Silver, gilding, porcelain, multicolored painting over glaze, paper, print.

41.3 × 27.5 × 8.8 cm.

Marks: Petersburg, "84", master: "P. U.", "M. K/1834".

Inv. No. PDMP 214, 214/1-dm.

Cover in gilded silver frame with porcelain insets: on the center medallion is the composition "Resurrection of Christ"; on the bevel squares, the Evangelists are depicted.

~ 117 ~

LITURGICAL SET

1834.

Petersburg, Russia.

Craftsman's monogram: "P. U." (silver).

Imperial Porcelain Factory.

Silver, chasing, gilding, porcelain, multicolored painting over glaze;
case: wood, leather, moire (watered silk), velvet.

Case: 53 × 28.5 cm.; chalice: H. 24.4 cm.; altartop crucifix:
L. 23.3 cm.; paten: H. 11.8 cm.; star-cover: 12.6 × 12.6 × 11.5 cm.;
communion spoon: 18.3 × 3.2 cm.; plates: diameter 12.4.

Mark: Petersburg, "84", master: "P. U.", "M. K/1834".

Inv. No. PDMP 203-210-dm

In the case there are seven items: a chalice with four
porcelain insets; an altartop crucifix; star-cover and a
communion spoon with porcelain insets; a paten; and
two plates.

~ 118 ~

TABERNACLE

1834.

Petersburg, Russia.

Craftsman's monogram: "P. U."

Silver, gilding, chasing.

H. 46.5 cm.

Marks: Petersburg, "84", master: "P. U.", "M. K/1834".

Inv. No. PDMP 213-dm.

In the form of a gothic chapel.

— 119 —

"HOLIDAY" ICON

Painting: Russia, mid-19th century.
Setting: Petersburg, 1856.

P. Andrianov.

Icon: wood, oils, gilding.
Setting: silver, embossing, gilding.

53.8 × 44.9 cm.

Mark: Petersburg, "84", "P. ANDRIANOV", "E. B./1856".

Inv. No. PDMP 1061/1, 2-dm.

On the center panel, the composition "The Last Supper"; surrounding it are 15 scenes depicting holidays;
the setting is adorned with plant ornament; at the corners are the four Evangelists; in the center is the composition "Ascension of Christ."

~ 120 ~

MITRE

1850–1870.

Petersburg, Russia.

Velvet, galloon lace, stitching, mother-of-pearl, painting, silver,
aquamarines, glass.

H. 28.8 cm.

Inv. No. PDMP 1096-dm

Of red velvet, with gold stitching and four miniatures
painted on mother-of-pearl, with depictions of Jesus
Christ, John the Baptist, Mary, and the Crucifixion.

~ 121 ~

VESTMENTS OF A DEACON (SURPLICE, ORARION)

1750–1800.

Russia.

Brocade, silk.

H. of surplice: 148 cm.
H. of orarion: 293 cm.

Inv. No. PDMP 473, 477-bk.

Festive deacon's vestments made of gilded brocade with flower ornament. Vestments of clergy of the Orthodox Church in Russia, including the felonion, the surplice, the sakkos, and other items, were made in sets from one fabric for the staff of an entire parish. They were usually sewn in monastery workshops and were richly adorned with gold stitching, precious stones, and paste (strass).

HISTORY OF PETERHOF THROUGH ART

The iconography of Peterhof is extraordinarily rich. The first depictions of Peterhof date from the early 18th century. As a rule, these are drawings by Peter I himself or by the first architects to construct Peterhof.

The graphic arts of the second half of the 18th century are more varied in subject and color scheme. Some of the most interesting materials of that time include the axonometric plans of French mathematician and cartographer P.-A. de Saint-Hilaire, which were commissioned from him by the Empress Catherine II. Today these sketches allow us not only to appreciate the extremely high mastery of the builders of past centuries, but also to benefit from the labors of the French mathematician in the project of restoration of parts of Peterhof that were destroyed during the years of the Second World War. It is impossible to overestimate the historical significance of these drawings by Saint-Hilaire.

One encounters a completely different image of the imperial residence than St. Hilaire's in a series of engravings from the end of the 18th and beginning of the 19th centuries. This series consists of a few pages among which are pictures of the Marly Palace, the Hermitage Cascade, and other views of the Lower and Upper Parks. They were executed by masters of the landscape engraving class of the Petersburg Academy of Arts. One of the plates, cut by S. F. Galaktionov, depicts the Italian Fountain in the Lower Gardens at Peterhof. From this same series, an engraving by another graduate of the Academy of Arts, A. G. Ukhtomsky, "View of the Great Pool in the Upper Gardens at Peterhof," was executed after a picture by S. Shchedrin.

The graphic pages of the Academicians, with their astoundingly meticulous selection of representations of views of Peterhof, have been accepted as classic depictions of the summer capital of Russia. These views have more than once been reproduced, in different versions, on porcelain, in drawings, in embroidery, etc.

In the mid-19th century, when Peterhof flourished, artists displayed an even greater interest in the seaside gardens of the Russian emperors. It is at that time that many works appear, both depictions of cozy corners of the park and watercolors executed by painters by order of the Emperor, Master of the summer residence, for documentary purposes. Among the latter are a set of views of interiors of the Cottage and of the Farm Palace by the painter E. P. Hau, a virtuoso master of watercolor technique.

The interiors of another palace, the Private Dacha, so entranced the Emperor that he handed over the challenge of visually capturing them to yet another brilliant watercolorist, Luigi Premazzi, of Italian extraction. Bright, and rendered by an artist who is clearly openly savoring the rich appointment of the rooms executed according to the plans of architect A. I. Stackenschneider, these paintings captured, once and for all, the impression of that which has now become history. The Private Dacha, destroyed during the years of World War II, survives now only in the works of artists.

In the mid-19th century, painters were attracted not only by the newly-appearing palaces and parks. They were always drawn to artifacts of Peter's time as well. Nicholas I himself was a passionate admirer of his great-grandfather. This is perhaps why, to please the Emperor, or perhaps by his own inspiration, E. Hau made a painting of the Oak Office in the Great Palace, which had preserved the atmosphere and appearance of the early 18th century. And, of course, the renowned seaside balustrade near Monplaisir Palace continued to attract artists. It is here that, even today, Peterhof opens onto a magnificent panorama of the Gulf of Finland, with a view of Petersburg and the

The Great Palace and the Great Cascade (item #137) at left

maritime fortress Kronstadt. Many reminiscences of the biographers of Peter I and Catherine the Great hearken back to this spot. Catherine, writing in her journal, repeatedly mentions her "morning coffee" on this terrace.

Outsiders were rarely admitted to Peterhof's private parks. On one foreigner, however, the well-known French seascape painter Theodor Gudin, was bestowed the honor of painting the favorite residence of Nicholas I. When, in the spring of 1841, he met with the Russian Tsar in Warsaw, Gudin was invited "to embark for Russia together with His Majesty." His paintings of views of Alexandria both manifest the hand of a fine artist and, at the same time, capture the poetry of the romantic park.

And yet, throughout the years, the most attractive point for artists continued to be the famous view of the Great Cascade and Great Palace, described in so many memoirs, accounts, and journals. Even the prominent Russian seascape painter I. K. Aivazovsky could not remain indifferent to it and, deserting for a time his beloved theme of seascapes, he devoted to this view his painting "The Great Peterhof Palace."

The splendor of Peterhof has always not only enchanted its numerous guests, but has also sparked creative inspiration in the hearts of true artists. In the early 20th century, one singer of praise to Peterhof, the famous art historian and artist Alexander Benois, wrote: "Marvelously beautiful and lyrical is Peterhof, a living witness to the most brilliant and the most tragic pages of Russian history, and in itself a wonderful artistic monument to the art of the 18th century, towards the creation of which the greatest masters of that time devoted their efforts."

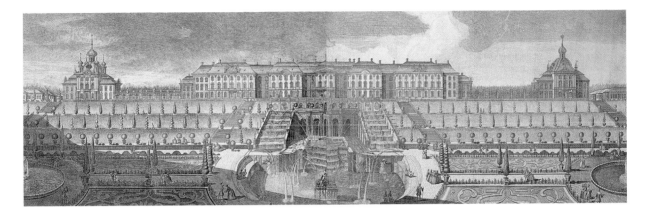

— 122 —

GREAT PALACE AT PETERHOF

1761.

Nikita Chelnakov (1734–1789), Prokopii Artemiev (1736–1803).

From a drawing by M. Makhaev (c. 1717–1770). 1756.

Under the picture to the left: Drawn by M. M. Makhaev;
to the right: Engravers: N. Chelnakov and P. Artemiev
in St. Petersburg, Imperial Academy.

Engraving.

40.9 × 65.3 cm.

Inv. No. PDMP 222/1, 2-gr.

A panorama of the the floor of the Lower Park. The Great Cascade and Great Palace are in the form they acquired after the rebuilding of the ceremonial summer residence according to plans of architect F.-B. Rastrelli realized in 1747–1755.

Pierre Antonio de Saint-Hilaire (?–1780). A representative of the French school of cartographic art, engineer, mathematician. Worked in Holland, where he made axonometric schemes of the Hague. In 1764 he came to Russia. Catherine II, upon perusing the work of P. A. de Saint-Hilaire, suggested that he create the same sort of maps of Saint Petersburg and its environs. He conducted axonometric measurements of Petersburg, Tsarskoe Selo, and Oranienbaum.

— 123 —

AXONOMETRIC MAP OF THE GREAT PALACE OF
PETERHOF, FROM THE SIDE OF THE LOWER PARK

1772–1773.

Pierre Antonio de Saint-Hilaire.

Petersburg, Russia.

French paper, ink, watercolor.

50 × 71 cm.

On the right, under the border, inscription: "Leve en.1772 et
Dessine en 1773 par P. A. De St. Hilaire Cap-e. Ing-e".

Inv. No. PDMP 4618/2-ar

GREAT CASCADE—the principal fountain structure of the Lower Park of Peterhof. Set on a slope at
the base of the Great Palace. Built in 1715–1735; some
changes in its decor were made in the 19th century.

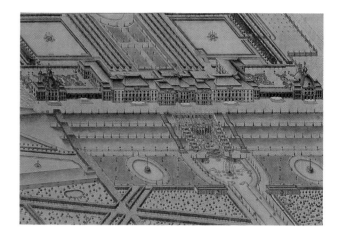

— 124 —

AXONOMETRIC MAP OF THE GREAT PALACE
OF PETERHOF, FROM THE SIDE
OF THE UPPER GARDENS

1772–1774.

Pierre Antonio de Saint-Hilaire.

Petersburg, Russia.

French paper, ink, watercolor.

50 × 71 cm.

On the right, under the border, inscription: "Leve en.1772 et Dessine
en 1773 par P. A. De St. Hilaire Cap-e. Ing-e".

Inv. No. PDMP 4618/3-ar.

THE UPPER GARDENS at Peterhof are a part of the
palace-park complex. The gardens are situated in front
of the southern facade of the Great Palace of Peterhof.
Planned as a "regular" (French) park in 1716–1723,
adorned with fountains, flower beds, and copses.

(Photo not available.)

— 125 —

AXONOMETRIC MAP OF THE MONPLAISIR
PALACE WITH SIDE BUILDINGS AND GARDENS,
FROM THE SIDE OF THE LOWER PARK

1772–1774.

Pierre Antonio de Saint-Hilaire.

Petersburg, Russia.

French paper, ink, watercolor.

50 × 71 cm.

On the right, under the border, inscription: "Leve en.1772 et Dessine en
1774 par P. A. De St. Hilaire Cap-e. Ing-e".

Inv. No. PDMP 4618/5-ar

MONPLAISIR in the Lower Park of Peterhof was
built in 1714–1722, presumably according to plans
drawn up by A. Shliuter for Peter I (the Great), who
would live there during his stays at Peterhof. The date
on which the construction of Monplaisir was begun is
considered the date of the founding of the ceremonial summer residence of the Russian Emperors near
Petersburg. The Monplaisir Palace compound included guest galleries, the Catherine Wing, the Bath
and Kitchen Halls, the Kofishenskaia (pavilion for
preparation and consumption of coffee) and
Tafeldeker (for storage of clean table linen) buildings,
and the Assembly Hall.

(Photo not available.)

— 126 —

AXONOMETRIC MAP OF THE "PYRAMID"
FOUNTAIN IN THE LOWER PARK OF PETERHOF

1772–1774.

Pierre Antonio de Saint-Hilaire.

Petersburg, Russia.

French paper, ink, watercolor, silk.

50 × 71 cm.

On the right, under the border, inscription: "Leve en.1772 et Dessine
en 1774 par P. A. De St. Hilaire Cap-e. Ing-e".

Inv. No. PDMP 4618/9-ar.

The "PYRAMID" is a fountain in the Lower Park. It
was built according to the designs of architect N.
Michetti in 1721–1724. The author of the water-delivery
system is fountain master P. Soilem. In 1799 the
fountain was rebuilt and its wooden decorations were
replaced by marble ones.

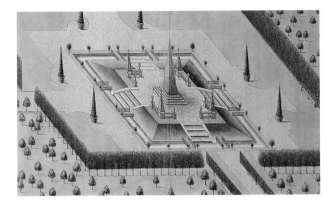

— 127 —

AXONOMETRIC MAP
OF THE "ADAM" FOUNTAIN AND TRELLISES

1772.

Pierre Antonio de Saint-Hilaire.

Petersburg, Russia.

French paper, ink, watercolor, silk.

50 × 71 cm.

On the right, under the border, inscription: "Leve en.1772 et
Dessine par P. A. De St. Hilaire Cap-e. Ing-e".

Inv. No. PDMP 4618/8-ar.

"ADAM" is a fountain in the Eastern part of Peterhof's
Lower Park. Built in 1721. Plans for the fountain
were developed by architects N. Michetti and I.
Braunstein, with the participation of Peter I himself.
The sculptures of Adam and (on the paired fountain)
Eve were created in 1718 in Venice by the Italian master
Giovanni Bonazza. The waterworks was designed
by fountain master P. Sualem. The trellised gazebos
around the fountain were built in the 1830s.

(Photo not available.)

— 128 —

AXONOMETRIC MAP OF THE "CHESSBOARD
MOUNTAIN" CASCADE AND THE ROMAN
FOUNTAINS WITH THE ADJACENT PART
OF THE LOWER PARK

1772–1774.

Pierre Antonio de Saint-Hilaire.

Petersburg, Russia.

French paper, ink, watercolor.

50 × 71 cm.

On the right, under the border, inscription: "Leve en.1772
et Dessine en 1774 par P. A. De St. Hilaire Cap-e. Ing-e".

Inv. No. PDMP 4618/10-ar.

"CHESSBOARD MOUNTAIN" is a cascade in the
Lower Park. It was repeatedly rebuilt during the
course of the 18th and 19th centuries. Architects I.
Braunstein, N. Michetti, and A. LeBlond took part in
its creation. The original wooden figures of dragons
on the summit of the cascade were replaced in 1864
by lead ones executed according to designs by N.
Benois. The Rome Fountains are located in the floor
area in front of the Chessboard Mountain Cascade.
Built in the mid-18th century, they were remade by
architect V. Rastrelli.

(Photo not available.)

— 129 —

AXONOMETRIC MAP OF THE ORANGERY
IN PETERHOF'S LOWER PARK

1772–1774.

Pierre Antonio de Saint-Hilaire.

Petersburg, Russia.

French paper, ink, watercolor, silk.

50 × 71 cm.

On the right, under the border, inscription: "Leve en.1772
et Dessine en 1774 par P. A. De St. Hilaire Cap-e. Ing-e".

Inv. No. PDMP 4618/11-ar.

The ORANGERY is a stone building in the Lower
Park built in 1722–1724. It was rebuilt several times
during the 18th and 19th centuries. Destroyed during
World War II, it has been reconstructed.

(Photo not available.)

— 130 —

AXONOMETRIC MAP OF THE HERMITAGE PALACE
FROM THE SIDE OF THE LOWER PARK

1772–1775.

Pierre Antonio de Saint-Hilaire.

Petersburg, Russia.

French paper, ink, watercolor, silk.

50 × 71 cm.

On the right, under the border, inscription: "Leve et Dessine
par P. A. De St. Hilaire Cap-e. Ing-e".

Inv. No. PDMP 4618/4-ar.

The HERMITAGE is a pavilion in the western part of
the Lower Park built according to plans by architect I.
Braunstein in 1721–1724. In 1757, under the direction
of V. Rastrelli, the second floor hall was lined with
paintings. Catherine II arranged musical evenings and
literary readings in this intimate setting.

(Photo not available.)

— 131 —

AXONOMETRIC MAP OF THE MARLY PALACE,
FROM THE EASTERN SIDE, WITH ADJACENT
PARTS OF THE LOWER PARK.

Pierre Antonio de Saint-Hilaire.

Petersburg, Russia.

French paper, ink, watercolor, silk.

50 × 71 cm.

On the right, under the border, inscription: "Leve en.1772
et Dessine en 1774 par P. A. De St. Hilaire Cap-e. Ing-e".

Inv. No. PDMP 4618/6-AR.

MARLY is a palace in the western part of the Lower
Park, built in 1720–1723 by architect I. Braunstein on
commission from Peter I. The Marly Pond approaches
it from the east. An area of the park surrounding
Marly Palace is separated from the Gulf of Finland by
an artificial ridge—the Marly Rampart. On the southern slope, to the left of the Palace, is situated the
Marly Cascade (or Golden Mountain), built in
1722–1732 after a design by architects N. Michetti
and M. Zemtsov.

(Photo not available.)

— 132 —

AXONOMETRIC MAP OF THE "EVE" FOUNTAIN
WITH TRELLISES

1772.

Pierre Antonio de Saint-Hilaire.

Petersburg, Russia.

French paper, ink, watercolor, silk.

50 × 71 cm.

On the right, under the border, inscription: "Leve en.1772 et
Dessine par P. A. De St. Hilaire Cap-e. Ing-e".

Inv. No. PDMP 4618/7-ar.

"EVE" is a fountain in the western part of the Lower
Park. Built in 1726 as a pair to the "ADAM" fountain.

(Photo not available.)

— 133 —

VIEW OF THE MARLY PALACE
AND THE GOLDEN MOUNTAIN CASCADE
IN THE LOWER PARK AT PETERHOF

1805.

Stepan Galaktionov (1778/9–1854).

Engraving, etching.

51 × 66 cm.

Under the picture, to the left: Drawn from nature and
engraved by S. Galaktionov. View of Marly and
the Golden Mountain from the side of Parnassus, at Peterhof.
To His Imperial Majesty Alexander I. Sovereign Emperor
and Absolute Monarch of All Russia.

Inv. No. PDMP 212-gr.

A depiction of the Golden Mountain cascade in the
Lower Park, built from plans by architects N. Michetti
and M. Zemtsov in 1722–1732. On the right, on the
pond's shore, is the Marly Palace. In the park the Empress Elizabeth Alexeevna, wife of Alexander I, is
walking.

The Lower Park, which was originally designed on
the model of French "regular" gardens, had, by the
early 19th century, lost its original appearance. In the
18th century, by dispensation of Elizabeth II, who was
partial to English-style parks, trimming of the trees
was discontinued, which eventually brought the park
closer to a natural appearance.

~ 134 ~

VIEW OF THE ITALIAN FOUNTAIN
IN THE LOWER PARK AT PETERHOF

1804–1805.

Stepan Galaktionov.

From a drawing by Semyon Shchedrin (1745–1804).

Engraving, etching.

72 × 93.5 cm.

Under the illustration, to the left: Drawn by Acad. Art
Adjunctant Rector S. Shchedrin. Engr: S. Galaktionov.
To His Imperial Majesty Alexander I. Sovereign Emperor
and Absolute Monarch of All Russia.

Inv. No. PDMP 2258-zh.

The Italian Fountain in the Lower Park was built in
1721–1722 from plans by architect N. Michetti and
Italian Fountain masters the Brothers Barratini. This
was the first fountain to function on the day of the
ceremonial opening of the summer residence, August
15, 1723.

(Photo not available. Work under restoration.)

~ 135 ~

VIEW OF THE GREAT POOL IN THE UPPER
GARDEN OF PETERHOF

Early 19th century.

Andrei Ukhtomsky (1770—after 1858).

From a drawing by S. Shchedrin.

Engraving, etching.

72 × 93.6 cm.

Under the illustration, to the left: Drawn by Acad. Art Adjunctant
Rector S. Shchedrin. Engr: A. Ukhtomsky.

Inv. No. PDMP 2256-zh.

The principal fountain in the Upper Garden, Nep-
tune, was created in 1798 by order of Emperor Paul I.
In the center of the Great Pool, a sculptural group,
made by German masters C. Ritter and G. Schweigger
in the mid-17th century, was placed.

(Photo not available. Work under restoration.)

THE GREAT PALACE AND THE GREAT CASCADE

1837.

Ivan Aivazovsky (1817–1900).

Oil on canvas.

44.2 × 62.3 cm.

On the lower right, a monogram of letters "I" and "A".

Inv. No. PDMP 749-zh.

(Photo appears on page 116.)

— 138 —

OAK STUDY OF THE EMPEROR PETER I
IN THE GREAT PALACE

1852.

Edward Hau (1807–1870).

Paper, watercolor, white ground.

22.1 × 32 cm.

On the lower left, signature: EvdHau.

Inv. No. PDMP 144-ak.

The office owes its name to its carved oak panels, made from drawings by Nicolas Pineau in 1718–1720. The Oak Office was preserved during the 18th and 19th centuries as a relic linked to the memory of the first Russian emperor (Cat. No.s 183, 184).

(Photo not available. Work under restoration.)

— 136 —

THE COURT EXIT
FROM THE GREAT PALACE AT PETERHOF

1852.

Vasily Sadovnikov (1800–1879).

Paper, watercolor, white ground, ink.

30.3 × 39.6 cm.

Inv. No. PDMP 10-ak.

~ 139 ~

VIEW OF THE PICTURE HALL
OF THE GREAT PALACE

1855.

Luigi Premazzi (1814–1891).

Paper, pencil, watercolor, white ground.

26 × 32 cm.

Inv. No. PDMP 157-ak.

The Picture Hall was the central hall in the Great Palace even before its remodeling by architect Rastrelli in the mid-18th century. In 1764 the walls of the Hall were adorned by 368 paintings by P. Rotari, acquired by the Empress Catherine II.

— 140 —

BEDROOM OF THE EMPEROR PETER I
IN THE MONPLAISIR PALACE

1846.

Konstantin Ukhtomsky (1818–1881).

Paper, pencil, watercolor.

29.3 × 19.3 cm.

On the lower right, signature and date: SO … m … 1846.

Inv. No. PDMP 66-ak.

— 141 —

THE TERRACE OF MONPLAISIR

1843.

Johann Meier (1787–1858).

Paper, pencil, watercolor, white ground.

24.3 × 34.4 cm.

On the lower right, signature and date: J. J. Meier 1843.

Inv. No. PDMP 158-ak.

The view onto the Gulf of Finland from the terrace in front of the Monplaisir Palace. In the distance the Peterhof jetty in the Lower Park is visible, and on the horizon, the Kronstadt Fortress.

(Photo not available. Work under restoration.)

— 142 —

ALEXANDRIA PARK

1841.

Theodor Gudin (1804–1880).

Oil on canvas.

48.5 × 88.8 cm.

On the lower right, signature and date: T. Gudin.
Cottage 7/18 aout 1841.

Inv. No. PDMP 717-zh.

The painting depicts a panorama of the Alexandria Park, a view from the balcony of the Cottage Palace at sunset. Through the greenery of the trees, the Capella, built to the plans of K. F. Schinkel in 1831–1833, is visible, and beyond that, the cupola of the Great Palace.

Alexandria was the private residence of the Romanovs, originally designed to include a park, the Cottage Palace, and service buildings. Built to the design of the Scottish architect A. A. Menelaus. The park is named in honor of the wife of Nicholas I, Alexandra Feodorovna.

(Photo not available. Work under restoration.)

— 143 —

VIEW OF THE COTTAGE FROM THE SEA

1854.

Iossif Charlemagne (1824–1870).

Paper, pencil, watercolor, white ground.

13 × 18.5 cm.

Inv. No. PDMP 37/3-ak.

The Cottage Palace, like the entire Alexandria estate, was built in gothic style in 1826–1829 to designs by architect A. A. Menelaus. It was presented by Nicholas I to his spouse, Alexandra Feodorovna.

— 144 —

DRAWING ROOM OF THE EMPRESS ALEXANDRA
FEODOROVNA IN THE COTTAGE PALACE

1855.

Edward Hau.

Paper, pencil, watercolor.

27.9 × 36.8 cm.

On the bottom, signature and date: Alexandria Ed Hau 1855.

Inv. No. PDMP 25-ak.

Empress Alexandra Feodorovna's drawing room was located on the ground floor of the Cottage Palace. The room's decoration was designed by architect A. Menelaus in gothic style, and the majority of objects adorning the interior were similarly executed in that style (see section of catalogue entitled "Cottage Palace. Drawing Room of Alexandra Feodorovna").

(Photo not available. Work under restoration.)

— 145 —

THE FARM PALACE IN ALEXANDRIA PARK

1858.

Henri-Pierre Blanchard. (1805–1873).

Paper, pencil, watercolor, white ground.

30.3 × 46.7 cm.

On the lower left, signature and date: P Blanchard PetercHoff 1858.

Inv. No. PDMP 65-ak

The Farm was built in Alexandria Park in 1831 to the specifications of architect A. Menelaus, and was used for its intended purpose. Later, in the 1840s and 1850s, the building was rebuilt by architect A. Stackenschneider, who adapted it into a palace, which then became the summer residence, first of the Grand Duke Alexander Nikolaevich, subsequently the Emperor Alexander II. Here, in the Farm Palace, a document most important in the history of Russia was drafted: the Manifesto liberating the peasants.

— 146 —

BLUE OFFICE OF THE EMPEROR
ALEXANDER II IN THE FARM PALACE

1860.

Edward Hau.

Paper, pencil, watercolor, white ground.

24.4 × 34.3 cm.

On the lower left, signature and date: Academiker EdHau 1860.

Inv. No. PDMP 21-ak.

The Blue Office of Emperor Alexander II was located
on the palace's ground floor. The room was decorated
in gothic style.

— 147 —

STUDY OF THE EMPRESS
MARIA ALEXANDROVNA IN THE FARM PALACE

c. 1860.

Edward Hau.

Paper, pencil, watercolor, white ground.

27 × 30 cm.

On the lower left, signature: EdvHau.

Inv. No. PDMP 18-ak.

The office of the Empress Maria Alexandrovna was a
typical Biedermeier epoch interior featuring an abun-
dance of everyday objects.

— 148 —

THE PRIVATE DACHA
[SUMMERHOUSE] AT PETERHOF

1850.

Vasily Sadovnikov.

Paper, pencil, watercolor.

26.5 × 35.5 cm.

On the lower left, signature and date: Sadovnicoff 1850.

Inv. No. PDMP 3-ak.

"Her Imperial Majesty's Private Dacha" was built in the mid-18th century for Elizabeth Petrovna, the daughter of Peter I. In 1843 Emperor Nicholas I presented this estate to his son Alexander Nikolaevich. Here, on the site of Elizabeth's dacha, architect Andrei Stankenschneider erected a palace in a rococo style characteristic for the mid-18th century.

— 149 —

BATHROOM AT THE PRIVATE DACHA

1852.

Luigi Premazzi.

Paper, pencil, watercolor.

33.9 × 24.1 cm.

On the lower left, signature and date: Premazzi 52.

Inv. No. PDMP 6-ak.

— 150 —

RASPBERRY DRAWING ROOM
AT THE PRIVATE DACHA

Mid-18th century.

Edward Hau.

Paper, pencil, watercolor, white ground.

24.7 × 29.6 cm.

On the lower left, signature: Edv Hau.

Inv. No. PDMP 7-ak.

The Raspberry Drawing Room is a typical rococo-style interior.

(Photo not available. Work under restoration.)

‹ 151 ›

PLATTER FROM THE FARM PALACE SERVICE

1845–1881.

St. Petersburg, Russia.

Imperial Porcelain Factory.

Porcelain, multicolored painting
over glaze, gilding.

L. 28 cm.

Marks: green, under glaze: A II under a crown;
black inscription over glaze: Imperial English Palace
at Peterhof in 1847.

Inv. No. PDMP 871-f.

A picture of the English Palace at Peterhof. The English Palace and English Park were created at Peterhof near the primary area of the ceremonial summer residence by order of the Empress Catherine II. The palace, built to the designs of architect G. Quarenghi in the 1780s, was the main structure of the park, which was laid out in the "landscape" or "English" style of park-design characteristic of the time of Catherine II's reign. During the years of World War II the palace was destroyed.

The main body of this service were made in 1840–1841. It was intended for the Farm Palace in Alexandria Park. Along the border of the platter runs the monogram of the Grand Duke Alexander Nikolaevich, an "A" under a crown.

(Photo not available. Work under restoration.)

‹ 152 ›

TRAY FROM A TWO-PERSON SERVICE

1908.

St. Petersburg, Russia.

Imperial Porcelain Factory.

Porcelain, multicolored painting over glaze, gilding.

L. 43.5 cm.

Marks: green on unglazed bottom: A II 9 under a crown.

Inv. No. PDMP 874-f

With a depiction of the Royal Guards of the Ulan Regiment near the pylons of the gates to the Upper Garden. The pylons decorated the front entrance from the square to the Upper Garden.

— 153 —

PLATES FROM THE BABIGON SERVICE

1823–1824, 1892.

St. Petersburg, Russia.

Imperial Porcelain Factory.

Porcelain, multicolored painting over glaze, gilding.

D. 22 cm.

1. *No mark; on the underside a black inscription over glaze:*
   View of the Oak Fountain at Peterhof.

   Inv. No. PDMP 1647-f

   With a depiction of the "Little Oak" Fountain in the
   Lower Park of Peterhof.

2. *Green mark, under glaze:* A III 92 *under a crown; on the*
   underside a black inscription over glaze: Alexandria at
   Peterhof.

   Inv. No. PDMP 2264-f.

   With a depiction of the Cottage Palace.

3. *Mark:* A III 92 *under a crown; on underside, a black in-*
   scription over glaze: Church at Alexandria near Peterhof.

   Inv. No. PDMP 2265-f

   With a picture of the Gothic Capella in the Alexandria
   Park. The Gothic Capella was built according to a design
   by architect K. F. Schinkel in 1828–1831 for the family
   of the Emperor Nicholas I.

4. *Black inscription over glaze:* View of the Palace at Strelna.

   Inv. No. PDMP 2266-f.

   Depicts the Strelna Palace.

The palace at the village of Strelna, located not far
from Peterhof, was founded by Peter I and was to
have become the center of the ceremonial summer
residence. Soon thereafter, it was decided to relocate
the residence to Peterhof. Subsequently, the palace
was rebuilt and belonged first to the Grand Duke
Konstantin Pavlovich, son of the Emperor Paul I, and
later to the Grand Duke Konstantin Nikolaevich, son
of the Emperor Nicholas I.

The Babigon service was made in 1823–1824. It was
intended for the Great Peterhof Palace. Part of the service was transferred in 1857 to the Belvedere Palace
on the Babigon Heights near Peterhof. It was at that
time that the service was named "Babigon," after the
location. The items are painted with gold ornament
on a white and gray background; some of the plates
feature, on the bottom surface, depictions of views of
the Petersburg environs.

— 154 —

VASE

1815–1818.

St. Petersburg, Russia.

Imperial Porcelain Factory.

Shape designed by architect A. N. Voronikhin (1759–1814).

Drawings after engravings by S. F. Galaktionov and K. V. Chesky
(1776–1813) from originals by S. F. Shchedrin (1745–1804).

Porcelain, monochromatic printing over glaze.

H. 44 cm.

Inv. No. PDMP 3115-f

In the form of an urn, with handles in the forms of sitting Naiades; on both sides of the body of the vase,
printed depictions of the Italian Fountain in the
Lower Park at Peterhof and of the Pil-Tower in
Pavlovsk Park. The printed drawings on the vase are
rare examples of the use of this technique at the Imperial Russian Porcelain Factory. The technique of
printing on porcelain was introduced here during the
reign of Emperor Alexander I in 1814–1815, However,
as a means of decorating objects, it did not take root at
the Imperial Porcelain Factory, as the artistic virtues
of printing on porcelain were far inferior to those of
multicolored hand painting.

— 155 —

BOTTLE BUCKETS OF THE GURIEV SERVICE

1809–1816.

St. Petersburg, Russia.

Imperial Porcelain Factory.

Porcelain, multicolored painting over glaze, gilding.

H. 20 cm.

1. Inv. No. PDMP 3159-f
   With a depiction of the Marly Palace in the Lower Park.

2. Inv. No. PDMP 3162-f
   With a depiction of the terrace of the Monplaisir Palace.

— 156 —

PLATE

First quarter of the 19th century.

St. Petersburg, Russia.

Imperial Porcelain Factory.

Porcelain, multicolored painting over glaze, gilding.

D. 21.1 cm.

Black inscription over glaze: View of Marly in Peterhof Garden.

Inv. No. PDMP 1656-f.

With a painted image of the Marly Palace in the Lower Park.

(Photo not available. Work under restoration.)

— 157 —

CUP WITH SAUCER

1855–1881.

St. Petersburg, Russia.

Imperial Porcelain Factory.

Porcelain, multicolored painting over glaze, gilding.

H. of cup: 9 cm.; D. of saucer: 16 cm.

Marks: green, under glaze: A II 8 under a crown.

Inv. No. KP vr. khr. 1333/1,2

On the cup is a painted image of the Great Palace and Great Cascade in the Lower Park.

(Photo not available. Work under restoration.)

— 158 —

CUP WITH SAUCER

1855–1881.

St. Petersburg, Russia.

Imperial Porcelain Factory.

Porcelain, multicolored painting over glaze, gilding.

H. of cup: 9 cm.; D. of saucer: 16 cm.

Marks: green under glaze: A II 8 under a crown.

Inv. No. PDMP 873/1, 2-f

On the cup is a painted image of the Cottage Palace.

(Photo not available. Work under restoration.)

MONPLAISIR PALACE
Art Gallery

Two picture galleries, at the eastern and western sides of the palace, were created by order of the Emperor Peter I expressly for the housing of the picture collection. This was the first picture gallery in Russia devoted to the work of West European masters, and the work in it was collected by Peter the Great himself.

The collection consisted, for the most part, of works by Dutch and Flemish masters. Such were the tastes of the Lord of Monplaisir. The primary source of his acquisitions was auction sales in Amsterdam, which Peter visited, the artists themselves often aiding him in making his purchases. The Tsar was particularly fond of seascapes. The paintings were mounted in strict black frames. In the main Ceremonial Hall and the two galleries, for purposes of displaying the painting collection, specially designed housings were cut directly into the wooden paneling of the walls.

At the exhibition, the Eastern Gallery of Monplaisir Palace has been reproduced.

The Eastern Gallery at Monplaisir Palace at left

— 159 —

A CORNER OF A SEASIDE CITY

1703.

Frans van der Horn
(end of 17th century–early 18th century; Dutch).

Oil on canvas.

63 × 79 cm.

At lower center, signature: Frans v d Horn 1703.

Inv. No. PDMP 418-zh.

Painting of a corner of the Dutch city Zaandam, in which Peter the Great worked as a carpenter in the shipyards while living incognito in the home of a blacksmith.

~ 160 ~

SHIPS AT A QUIET MOORING

c. 1664–1665.

Willem van de Velde II Junior (1633–1707; Dutch).

Oil on canvas.

63.7 × 80.5 cm.

At lower center, signature: W v Velde.

Inv. No. PDMP 416-zh.

The painting depicts the Netherlands' navy fleet near the shore of Western Africa.

— 161 —

HUNTING TROPHIES

Philipp Hamilton (1664–1750; Flemish).

Oil on canvas.

65.8 × 85 cm.

Inv. No. PDMP 507-zh.

— 162 —
CAVALRY ENGAGEMENT
Carel Breydel (1677–1678; Flemish).
Oil on canvas.
55.3 × 75 cm.
Inv. No. PDMP 494-zh.

— 163 —

VESSELS AT A CITY MOORING
Adam Silo (1674–1757; Dutch).
Oil on canvas.
54 × 70.3 cm.
On the lower right, signature: Adam Silo.
Inv. No. PDMP 498-zh.

— 164 —

ORIENTAL WHARF

Carel Fieve (second half of the 17th century; Flemish).

Oil on canvas.

64 × 74.6 cm.

On the lower right, signature: Cfieveft.

Inv. No. PDMP 508-zh.

~ 165 ~

THE DESTRUCTION OF SODOM

Daniel van Heil (1604–1664; Flemish).

Oil on canvas.

64 × 79.5 cm.

Inv. No. PDMP 528-zh.

Biblical subject. The righteous man Lot, with his wife
and daughters, flees from Sodom, the city destroyed
by God as punishment for the sins of its residents.

— 166 —

CITY WHARF

1690.

Abraham Storck (c. 1636–c. 1710; Dutch).

Oil on canvas.

52 × 68 cm.

On the lower right, signature and date: A. Storck 1690.

Inv. No. PDMP 499-zh.

— 167 —

HUNT WITH FALCONS

Philips Wouwerman (c. 1619–1668; Dutch).

Oil on canvas.

58.7 × 77.8 cm.

On the lower left, monogram: PHLSW.

Inv. No. PDMP 527-zh.

— 168 —

SIEGE OF THE CITY OF TOURNAI
BY THE TROOPS OF LOUIS XIV

Adam Frans der Meulen (1632–1690; French).

Oil on canvas.

66 × 82.5 cm.

Inv. No. PDMP 505-zh

Illustrated is an episode from the Franco-Flemish wars
of the second half of the 17th century: the siege of the
Flemish city Tournai.

— 169 —

ARCHITECTURAL FANTASY

1704.

Jan van der Straeten (before 1660–1729; Flemish).

Oil on canvas.

57.5 × 83 cm.

On the lower left, signature and date: Joan van der Straeten, 1704.

Inv. No. PDMP 405-zh

— 170 —

PALLAS ATHENA AND THE MUSES

Jan van Balen (1611–1654; Flemish).

Oil on canvas.

68.1 × 88 cm.

Inv. No. PDMP 385-zh.

The muses greet their protectress, Pallas Athena, the
goddess of wisdom, patron of the sciences and arts, on
Parnassus, near the Castelian Spring.

— 171 —

BACCHAE AND SATYRS

Giullio Carpioni (1611–1674; Italian).

Oil on canvas.

68 × 83 cm.

Inv. No. PDMP 617-zh.

The Bacchae (or Maenads) are priestesses of Bacchus. The Satyrs are a forest deities comprising Bacchus' retinue. Both Bacchae and Satyrs take part in Bacchus' orgiastic rites, called bacchanalia.

— 172 —

ANTIOCH AND STRATONIKA

Gasparo Diziani (1686–1767; Italian).

Oil on canvas.

62 × 85 cm.

Inv. No. PDMP 568-zh.

The basis of the subject of this painting is a legend about the love of the Syrian Tsar Selevk Antioch for his stepmother Stratonika.

The painting depicts the climactic moment when doctor Erasistratus discovers the reason for Antioch's illness by noticing the acceleration of the youth's pulse at the moment Stratonika appears.

CHAIR

1700–1720.

Russia (?).

Walnut, carving, embroidery.

H. 142 cm.

Inv. No. PDMP 60-mb.

On the carved cartouche of the chair-back is the crown and monogram of Peter I; on the crossbar is a two-headed eagle, the coat of arms of the Russian Empire.

One of a set of seven chairs belonging to the Emperor Peter I.

TABLE

1719–1725.

Germany.

Oak, walnut, intarsia, slate.

H. 72 cm.

On the interior side of the tabletop, inscription: "Hannover".

Inv. No. PDMP 100-mb.

A tabletop with a sheet of slate, lined around the perimeter with a set of inlaid, stylized heraldic compositions. On four turned legs connected by an X-shaped support.

Legend has it that Peter I personally participated in the table's manufacture.

WAISTCOAT OF PETER I

1700–1725.

Western Europe.

Linen, embroidery.

H. 96 cm.

Inv. No. PDMP 79-tk.

Of white linen fabric, decorated with plant pattern embroidered in a single hue.

— 176 —

CANDLESTICK

1719.

Russia.

Copper.

H. 31 cm.

On the base, date: "1719".

Inv. No. PDMP 88-mt.

For one candle, on a flat round base.

From the Planer-Tree Wood Office of the Marly Palace. Among the personal effects of Peter I.

— 177 —

INKPOT

1680–1700.

Russia.

Yellow copper.

H. of inkpot: 6.5 cm.;
H. of quill-holder: 18.5 cm.

Inv. No. PDMP 92-mt.

To be worn on a belt, with a quill-holder. Among the personal effects of the Emperor Peter I.

— 178 —

CAFTAN OF PETER I

1703–1717.

Russia.

Broadcloth, silk, embroidery with silk and gold thread.

H. 121 cm.

Inv. No. PDMP 71-tk.

Caftan of white fabric; on the left side of the chest, a stitched silver order of the Holy Apostle Andrei Pervozvanny, with the motto: "For faith and loyalty."

The Order of Andrei Pervozvanny was the first Russian Order, established by Peter I in 1699. Peter I himself became the seventh Cavalier of this Order, in recognition of his leadership in the seizure of two Swedish vessels at the mouth of the Neva River.

ASSEMBLY HALL

—•—

The ASSEMBLY HALL is part of the Monplaisir compound. By order of the Empress Catherine I, three stone buildings, intended to house a cookery and other services, were built in the eastern part of the small Monplaisir Garden. In 1747 architect B. F. Rastrelli received an order to remodel the Kitchen Hall into the Assembly Hall, where he installed seventeen tapestries woven during 1720–1740 at the Petersburg Tapestry Works, founded by Peter in 1716. Eight large tapestries were a Russian reinterpretation of a series of French Gobelin tapestries called "The Indian Rugs" (Teintur des Indes), executed from cartoons by Francois Desportes (1661–1743), who in turn borrowed these subjects from a series of tapestries of the same name executed according to cartoons by the 17th century Dutch artist Albert van der Eckhout (1610–1666). Nine other tapestries, woven according to sketches of P. Pillement, are ornamental wall hangings (for placing between windows) with depictions of personages from Italian folk comedy, "Commedia dell'arte", framed by flowers and shell ornament. The Assembly Hall, or, as it was sometimes called, the Carpet Hall, is the only surviving mid-18th century interior in which tapestries are the primary decorative element.

The exhibition presents some of the tapestry appointments from the Assembly Hall.

~ 179 ~

TAPESTRY

1720–1732.

Petersburg, Russia.

After cartoons by Philippe Pillement (1684–1730).

Wool, silk, weaving.

265 × 68 cm.

Inv. No. PDMP 1, 4, 5, 8-tk.

Four tapestries made in two parts: a lower, ornamental part with a stylized star in the center; and an upper part with a depiction of a basket with flowers, a Zephyr's head, and birds, on a light blue field (PDMP 1, 8-tk); and with a depiction of a "Commedia dell'arte" personage (PDMP 4, 5-tk).

~ 180 ~

TAPESTRY "ASIA"

1733–1740.

Petersburg, Russia.

From the series "Indian Rugs."

Wool, silk, weaving.

391 × 286 cm.

Inv. No. PDMP 14-tk.

Against a background of a tropical landscape, a tiger attacking a zebra, a crocodile, a llama, a rhinoceros, and other animals. In the 18th century this was described as "Lion breaks a horse."

~ 181 ~

TAPESTRY OF AFRICA

1733–1740.

Petersburg, Russia.

From the series "Indian Rugs."

Wool, silk, weaving.

285 × 285 cm.

Inv. No. PDMP 15, 17-tk.

Against a background of a tropical landscape, half-naked slaves carry a local king on a litter (Inv. No. PDMP 15-tk) and a black man shoots from a bow (Inv. No. PDMP 17-tk).

Note to No. 191–193: All the illustrations are framed in a fabric frame with ornament that includes a cartouche with the monograms of the Empresses Anna Ioannovna (Cat. No.s 191, 192) and Elizabeth Petrovna (Cat. No. 193).

~ 182 ~

CHAIR

1716–1724.

Russia.

Oak, carving, tapestry.

H. 111 cm.

Inv. No. PDMP 95, 95-mb

The chairs are upholstered in tapestry depicting stylized flowers, vines, and birds, woven at the Petersburg
Tapestry Works founded by Peter I.

One of six chairs that were in Monplaisir Palace in
the 18th century.

— 183 —

CARD TABLE

1760–1770.

Petersburg, Russia.

Master: Nikifor Vasiliev (?)

Pine, maple, knotty maple, inlay with various kinds of wood.

H. 73 cm.

Inv. No. PDMP 941-mb.

On four curved legs, one of which swings up, allowing for unfolding of the table. Square tabletop with semicircular projections on the corners for holding candlesticks during games; along each side of the tabletop are indentations for chips and coins. The surface is adorned with inlaid depictions of architectural landscapes; on the upper lid is a composition: "Arcadian shepherds."

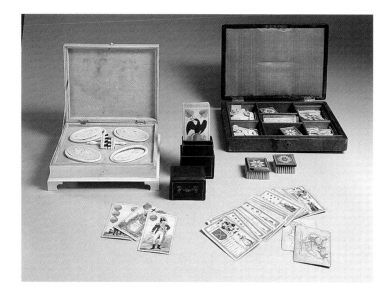

— 184 —

BOX WITH CHIPS FOR CARD GAMES

Early 19th century.

Russia.

Ivory, carving.

H. 7 cm.

Inv. No. PDMP 534, 534/1-6-bk.

Ivory box with carved ornament on the lid; inside, four carved oval baskets with chips of the different suits: clubs, diamonds, spades, and hearts, and with two little brushes for cleaning chalk marks from the card table.

— 185 —

BOX WITH CHIPS FOR CARD GAMES

1830–1840.

Russia.

Wood, ivory, leather, beads, glass.

H. 4 cm.

Inv. No. PDMP 540, 540/1-8-bk.

Brown leather box with a beaded inset in the lid depicting playing cards. Inside the box fit four smaller boxes with ivory chips of club, diamond, spade, and heart suits, and four brushes decorated with ornamental beaded insets.

— 186 —

CHIPS FOR CARD GAMES

1700–1710.

France.

Tortoiseshell, mother-of-pearl, gold, pique.

3.5 × 2.3 cm.

Inv. No. PDMP 1031-1035-dm, 410-469-bk.

Tortoiseshell, with inlaid suits in mother-of-pearl. Values marked in gold incrustation; two cross suits, two spades, one diamond; values from 10 to 50.

8 round and 8 long tortoiseshell chips; suits marked with inlaid mother-of-pearl; four chips for each suit.

Items shown on page 161.

— 187 —

PLAYING CARDS: "GEOGRAPHIC CARDS
FOR YOUNG PEOPLE"

1827–1831.

Petersburg, Russia.

Card Factory of the Imperial Boarding School.

Konstantin Gribanov (1797–?).

Cardboard, print from etchings, colored with watercolors.

9.6 × 6.5 cm.

Inv. No. PDMP 470/1-38-pg.

These cards were intended for the Lancaster schools; they appeared in Russia in the early 19th century and were printed after drawings by K. Gribanov, with the support of the Empress Maria Feodorovna and the Emperor Nicholas I. On the back of each card was a geographical map corresponding to an administrative region of Russia, with a list of all its cities, names of neighboring territories, and distances from the main city of the province to St. Petersburg and Moscow. The faces of the cards feature drawings of actual playing cards of the "French" type, the coat of arms of the land (or so-called province), and folk costumes of that region, as well as a list of its primary towns.

A similar deck of cards was kept in the Cottage Palace.

— 188 —

PLAYING CARDS

First quarter of the 19th century.

Germany.

Card stock, colored print.

10.1 × 6 cm.

Inv. No. PDMP 2262, 2262/1-33-gr.

These cards are dedicated to the Napoleonic Wars: in particular to the campaign of 1813–1814 against Napoleon's France, from the signing of an agreement between Russia and Prussia until the surrender of Paris and the abdication of Napoleon and the battle at Waterloo. Military figures and attributes of military men and the places and times of battles are indicated together with the playing cards' suits.

— 189 —

BEZIK

19th century.

Russia.

Wood, ivory.

H. 1 cm.

Inv. No. 672-bk.

Bezik was a card game beloved at the 18th-century French Court. In the mid-19th century it again came into fashion in Europe. In Russia, special cards (beginning with nines, and in special covers) were issued for playing bezik. From two to four players could participate in each game, and great skill was required to play.

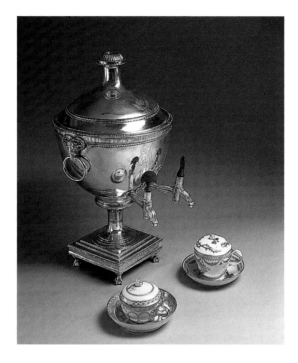

~ 190 ~

TWO CUPS WITH LIDS AND SAUCERS

1764–1796.

Petersburg, Russia.

Imperial Porcelain Factory.

Porcelain, colorless glaze, gilding.

H. of cup: 10 cm.; d. of saucer: 14.2 cm.

Blue marks, under glaze: E II

Inv. No. PDMP 3441/1, 2; 3442/1, 2-f

Decorated with a gold monogram of the Empress Catherine II. Made for her personal use.

GREAT STAIRCASE

Designed by architect F. B. Rastrelli as part of a more general expansion of the palace in the mid-18th century. The principal decorative elements of the Great Staircase were gilded, carved shell ornament, vases with flowers, and sculptures. The varied decor: multicolored painting with depictions of garlands of flowers, cupids holding the Empress' monogram, the carved allegorical figures of the portal and its imperial crown, the ceiling decorated with paintings on the theme of spring—all this was meant to glorify Elizabeth Petrovna, under whom "life is reborn and the sciences and arts flourish."

An important part of the carved design were four female figures personifying the four seasons of the year: spring, summer, autumn, and winter.

~ 191 ~

SCULPTURE "WINTER"

1751.

Russia.

After a design by architect Bartolomeo Rastrelli (1700–1771).

Linden wood, carving, gilding.

H. 177 cm.

Inv. No. PDMP 1232-mb.

The sculpture is part of a composition entitled "Seasons of the Year" that graces the upper landing of the Great Staircase. Carved in the image of a female figure muffling herself in a coat and warming herself at the fire of a brazier.

WHITE DINING ROOM

— • —

The interior of the White Dining Room of the Great Palace was newly renovated in the 1770s by order of Catherine II and according to the plans of architect Y. Felten. Here state dinners were held, grand and splendid ceremonial events that lasted several hours. Sometimes several hundred people participated in them. For such events, colossal dinner services consisting of several thousand pieces were brought from Europe. One "cream-colored," glazed porcelain service may serve as an example: it was commissioned by Catherine II in 1770 from the English factory "Etruria," founded by D. Wedgwood. The items in the service were adorned with violet-colored painted flowers and "husk" garlands, whence the service takes its name, the Husk Service.

As a rule, after receptions in the palace, many hundreds of items would be missing. For example, during the summer months of three years only, more than thirty-five thousand items were broken. It was necessary to constantly reorder more dishes from abroad. In 1822, however, a ban was introduced prohibiting the import of items of foreign manufacture. This edict was supposed to encourage the development of the domestic ceramics industry. After that time, supplementary and replacement items made by Russian enterprises appeared as parts of these services.

At the exhibition, a portion of the interior of the White Dining Room of the Great Palace of Peterhof has been reproduced, including a table set with a service commissioned by Catherine the Great.

Items on pages 168–173 are found in The White Dining Room shown on page 166.

⌐ 192 ⌐

ITEMS FOR SERVING 12 PERSONS
FROM THE "HUSK SERVICE"

3 SOUP PLATES

1770.

Porcelain: Staffordshire, England.
"Etruria" Factory.

Painting: London, England. "Decorating Studios."

Porcelain, monochromatic painting over glaze.

D. 25 cm.

Marks in pottery: WEDGWOOD.

Inv. No.s PDMP 451, 453, 454-f.

⌐ · ⌐

3 SOUP PLATES

1831–1842.

Russia, village of Mor'e, Schlusselburg uyezd
(administrative unit) of St. Petersburg province.

S. Ya. Poskochin Factory.

Porcelain, monochromatic painting over glaze.

D. 25.2 cm.

Marks in pottery: S P.

Inv. No.s PDMP 449, 450, 452-f.

⌐ · ⌐

6 SOUP PLATES

c. 1835.

Russia, village of Sablino, Tsarskoe Selo uyezd
(administrative unit) of St. Petersburg province.

Otto Factory.

Porcelain, monochromatic painting over glaze.

D. 24.5 cm.

Marks in pottery: L:O

Inv. No.s PDMP 444-446, 457, 460, 462-f.

⌐ · ⌐

12 WATERDISHES FOR WARMING FOOD

1830s.

Russia.

Unknown factory.

Porcelain, monochromatic painting over glaze.

D. 20.3 cm.

Marks in pottery: Old Russian letter "feta"

Inv. No.s PDMP 516-519, 522, 523, 525-527, 530, 534, 536-f.

12 FLAT PLATES

1770.

Porcelain: Staffordshire, England.
"Etruria" Factory.

Painting: London, England. "Decorating Studios."

Porcelain, monochromatic painting over glaze.

D. 25 cm.

Marks in pottery: WEDGWOOD

Inv. No.s PDMP 466, 487-489-f.

⌐ · ⌐

6 FLAT DESSERT PLATES

1770.

Porcelain: Staffordshire, England.
"Etruria" Factory.

Painting: London, England. "Decorating Studios."

Porcelain, monochromatic painting over glaze.

D. 22.1 cm.

Inv. No.s PDMP 491-496-f.

⌐ · ⌐

6 DESSERT PLATES

1850s.

St. Petersburg, Russia.

F. F. Gunter Factory

Porcelain, monochromatic painting over glaze.

D. 23.2 cm.

On one plate, mark in pottery: in an oval,
inscription "* GUNTER * S. P. B."

Inv. No.s PDMP 498, 500, 504, 506, 509, 510-f.

⌐ · ⌐

6 EGG CUPS

1770.

Porcelain: Staffordshire, England. "Etruria" Factory.

Painting: London, England. "Decorating Studios."

Porcelain, monochromatic painting over glaze.

H. 4 cm.

Inv. No.s PDMP 401-405-f.

SOUP TERRINE
Mid-19th century.
Russia.
Unknown factory.
Porcelain, monochromatic painting over glaze.
H. 23 cm.
Inv. No. PDMP 392-f.

2 TERRINES
End of 18th–early 19th century.
Porcelain: England, "Etruria" Factory
of D. Wedgwood.
Porcelain, monochromatic painting over glaze.
H. 21.7 and 16.8 cm.
Inv. No. PDMP 394, 419-f.

12 SHELLS FOR CREAM
1770.
Porcelain: Staffordshire, England. "Etruria" Factory.
Painting: London, England. "Decorating Studios."
Porcelain, monochromatic painting over glaze.
L. 28.8, 20.2, 33, 25.2, 32, and 29.5 cm.
On 5 of the shells, marks in pottery: WEDGWOOD
Inv. No.s PDMP 421-423, 415-f.

— • —

4 COVERED DISHES
1770.
Porcelain: Staffordshire, England. "Etruria" Factory.
Painting: London, England. "Decorating Studios."
Porcelain, monochromatic painting over glaze.
H. 11, 14.5, 15 cm.
On four dishes, marks in pottery: WEDGWOOD
Inv. No.s PDMP 417, 542, 441-f.

— • —

2 SAUCE BOATS
1830s.
Russia, village of Mor'e, Shlisselburg uyezd
(administrative unit) of St. Petersburg province.
S. Ya. Poskochin Factory.
Porcelain, monochromatic painting over glaze.
H. 13.3 cm.
Marks in pottery: S. P.
Inv. No.s PDMP 397, 398-f.

— • —

PLAT DE MENAGE (PICKLE DISH)
1770.
Porcelain: Staffordshire, England. "Etruria" Factory.
Painting: London, England. "Decorating Studios."
Porcelain, monochromatic painting over glaze.
H. 16 cm.
Inv. No.s PDMP 539-f.

— • —

2 FRUIT BASKETS
1770.
Porcelain: Staffordshire, England. "Etruria" Factory.
Painting: London, England. "Decorating Studios."
Porcelain, monochromatic painting over glaze.
H. 7.4 cm.
Inv. No.s PDMP 428, 431-f.

SAUCE TERRINE WITH LID AND SAUCER
1770.
Porcelain: England, "Etruria" Factory of D. Wedgwood.
Porcelain, monochromatic painting over glaze.
H. of sauce terrine: 11 cm.; H. of saucer: 2.5 cm.
Inv. No.s PDMP 409/1, 2-f.

— • —

SALAD BOWL
c. 1835.
Russia, village of Sablino, Tsarskoe Selo uyezd
(administrative unit) of St. Petersburg province.
Otto Factory.
Porcelain, monochromatic painting over glaze.
H. 7.7 cm.
Marks in pottery: L:OTTO
Inv. No. PDMP 411-f.

— • —

SUGAR BOWL WITH COVER AND SAUCER
1770.
Porcelain: Staffordshire, England. "Etruria" Factory.
Painting: London, England. "Decorating Studios."
Porcelain, monochromatic painting over glaze.
H. of sugar bowl: 15.3 cm.; H. Of saucer: 1.3 cm.
Marks in pottery of saucer: WEDGWOOD
Inv. No.s PDMP 408/1, 2-f.

— • —

SALT LADLES
1770.
Porcelain: Staffordshire, England. "Etruria" Factory.
Painting: London, England. "Decorating Studios."
Porcelain, monochromatic painting over glaze.
L. 7 cm.
Inv. No.s PDMP 406, 540, 541-f.

‿ 193 ‿

GLASS ITEMS FOR THE "HUSK SERVICE"

12 GLASSES
1750–1800.
Petersburg, Russia.
Imperial Glass Factory.
Colorless glass, gold painting.
H. 10 cm.
Inv. No.s PDMP 193, 194, 196-200, 202, 522-524, 527-st.

‿ . ‿

24 WINE GLASSES
1750–1800.
Petersburg, Russia.
Imperial Glass Factory.
Colorless glass, gold painting.
H. 12.5, 13.6, 14.2, 14.5 cm.
Inv. No.s PDMP 27, 149-1276-st.

6 CARAFES
1750–1800.
Petersburg, Russia.
Imperial Glass Factory.
Colorless glass, gold painting.
H. 21.5 cm.
Inv. No.s PDMP 56, 142-144, 146, 1055-st.

‿ . ‿

6 SHTOFS (RUSSIAN-STYLE 1.23 LITER BOTTLES)
1750–1800.
Petersburg, Russia.
Imperial Glass Factory.
Colorless glass, gold painting.
H. 15 cm.
Inv. No.s PDMP 120-123, 214, 493-st.

‿ 194 ‿

TWELVE KNIVES AND FORKS
1782.
Vienna, Austria.
Craftsman's monogram: "IIW".
Silver, gilding; porcelain, multicolored painting over glaze.
L. 21 cm. (fork) and 22 cm. (knife).
Marks: Vienna, "13", "1782", "IIW".
Inv. No. PDMP 1197-1220-dm.

Gilded, with porcelain handles painted with bouquets
of flowers.

‿ 195 ‿

TWO "GIRANDOLE" CANDLEHOLDERS
1760–1790.
Russia.
Gilded bronze, crystal.
H. 98 cm.
Inv. No.s PDMP 1561, 1562-mt.

For six candles, with crystal appointments.

— 196 —

COSTUME FROM THE WARDROBE
OF PRINCE POTEMKIN

1780–1790.

Russia.

Velvet, silver stitching, silk, sequins.

H. of caftan: 95 cm.
H. of camisole 57 cm.

Inv. No. PDMP 502, 766-tk.

The costume consists of three items: a caftan, a waist-coat, and short velvet trousers. The caftan is of black velvet with stylized plant ornamentation in silver stitching. The waistcoat is of white silk with matching stitching.

From the wardrobe of Prince Potemkin. Grigorii Alexandrovich Potemkin (1739–1791) was a Prince, General-Field Marshal of the Russian Army, and a prominent member of the government; one of the most influential people of his time. A favorite of the Empress Catherine II.

— 197 —

BUST OF THE EMPRESS CATHERINE II

1768–1775.

Carrara, Italy.

Giovanni Antonio Cybei (1706–1784).

Marble.

H. 73 cm.

Inv. No. PDMP 578-sk.

This bust was commissioned from the president of the Carrara Academy of Arts, G. Cybei, by Duke Alexei Orlov during one of his visits to Italy in 1768–1775. The bust was executed by the sculptor in the absence of his model, with the help only of painted depictions of the Empress.

CATHERINE WING

Bedroom of Alexander I

The sleeping quarters of Alexander I were located in the Catherine Wing of Monplaisir Palace. The wing was rebuilt by architect B.-F. Rastrelli in the mid-18th century for the daughter of Peter the Great, Empress Elizabeth Petrovna. Until her accession to the throne, Catherine I (the Great) lived here for almost 15 years. By her orders, the interiors were redecorated by Italian architect G. Quarenghi. In the early 19th century, the grandson of Catherine, the Emperor Alexander I, stayed in the palace. At that same time the room's decor was augmented with Empire style wall painting.

— 198 —

DEATH OF EURIDICA

End of the 17th century.

Unknown French artist.

Oil on canvas.

110.7 × 143.5 cm.

Inv. No. PDMP 1085-zh.

The subject of this painting is from Greek mythology. Euridica, wife of the Thracian singer Orpheus, was dancing a round dance with nymphs when a snake bit her.

Items on pages 176–179 are found in the Bedroom of Alexander I.

⌐ 199 ¬

BED

1810s.

Russia.

Red wood, veneering, carving.

H. 160 cm.

Inv. No. PDMP 776-mb.

In the shape of a boat, on a rectangular base, decorated with carved plant ornament.

⌐ 200 ¬

LINEN BASKET

1820s.

Russia.

Red wood, veneering, carving, silk.

H. 133 cm.

Inv. No. PDMP 1376-mb

Used for storing bedding during the day.

⌐ 201 ¬

SMALL TABLE

c. 1800.

Petersburg, Russia.

Studio of Heinrich Gambs (1765–1831).

Red and black wood, veneer, brass.

H. 74 cm.

Inv. No. PDMP 1062-mb

Round tabletop with star-shaped brass ornamentation along the edge.

Gambs came to Russia from Germany in 1790. In 1795 he was received by Catherine II (the Great) "for Court work;" until the end of his days Gambs would work for the Imperial Court. He developed an overall design for the furnishings of the Cottage Palace at Peterhof.

⌐ 202 ¬

COMMODE-SECRETARY

1800s.

Russia.

Red wood, veneering, carving, bronze, gold leaf.

H. 103.5 cm.

Inv. No. PDMP 1174-mb

With two drawers in the lower part; in the upper part, the folding board of the desk, upholstered in red leather. Front corners decorated with semi-female caryatid figures, drawer handles fashioned as lion heads.

⌐ 203 ¬

FOUR CHAIRS

1800–1810.

Russia.

Red wood, veneering, carving.

H. 90 cm.

Inv. No. PDMP 1446-1449-mb.

Chairs with round seats and half-oval shaped backs; decorated with carved ornament in the antique style.

⌐ 204 ¬

GERIDON TEA TABLE

1820s.

Russia.

Red wood, veneering, carving.

H. 77 cm.

Inv. No. PDMP 1670-mb.

On a column leg, with a raised border along the edge of the tabletop.

~ 205 ~

ITEMS FROM A TETE-A-TETE SERVICE:
TRAY, CREAM PITCHER, SUGAR BOWL WITH LID,
TWO CUPS WITH SAUCERS

1801–1825.

Petersburg, Russia.

Imperial Porcelain Factory.

Porcelain, multicolored painting over glaze, gilding.

H. of tray: 4.5 cm.; cream pitcher: 12.6 cm.; sugar bowl: 10.9 cm.;
cups: 6.3 cm.; saucers: 3.1 cm.

Blue marks under glaze: A under a crown

Inv. No. PDMP 6367-6371/1, 2-f.

Decorated with gold stripes on a white background;
between them, small branches with roses and garlands of leaves.

~ 206 ~

SCONCE WITH TWO ARMS

1760–1770.

Russia.

Bronze, gilding.

H. 47 cm.

Inv. No. PDMP 2385-mt.

In the form of a fluted column crowned by a vase.

~ 207 ~

TWO INCENSE BURNERS

End of 1790s.

France.

Bronze, gilding.

H. 35 cm.

Inv. No.s PDMP 651-mt, 652-mt.

In the form of an antique vase with a cover, with an
openwork band on the upper part; on a marble
pedestal.

~ 208 ~

PAIR OF STATUETTES; ZEPHYR AND FLORA

End of 1790s.

France.

Unknown sculptor.

Gilded and patinaed bronze, marble.

H. 46 and 44 cm.

Inv. No.s PDMP 916, 918-sk.

Statuettes of dark bronze mounted on a pedestal of colored marble with gilded detail.

From the sleeping quarters of the Emperor Alexander I in the Catherine Wing.

In ancient mythology, Zephyr personifies the warm western wind which brings rain; Flora is the goddess of flowers, youth and pleasure.

— 209 —

CLOCK

Late 1790s.

France.

Bronze, marble, gilding.

H. 54.5 cm.

Inv. No. PDMP 633-mt

In the form of a vase, on a marble base, with an open-work lid and handles shaped as caryatids.

— 210 —

TWO VASES

End of 1790s.

France.

Bronze, gilding, patina.

H. 10.7 cm.

Inv. No.s PDMP 645, 646-mt.

Dark bronze, in the form of a pitcher. On the body of the vases, a belt of relief work depicting children's bacchanalian scenes.

— 211 —

TWO CANDELABRAS

1800–1810.

Paris, France.

Louis-Stanislav Ravrio. (1783–1840).

Bronze, marble, gilding, patina.

H. 54.5 cm.

Along the edge of the base, signature: "L. RAVRIO BRONZIER A PARIS."

Inv. No.s PDMP 978, 979-mt.

Pantinaed bronze, with a female figure in antique attire in whose raised arms are gilded bronze branches.

— 212 —

CACHE-POT VASE

1820s.

France.

Bronze, gilding.

H. 38 cm.

Inv. No. PDMP 1095-mt.

Round, on three legs shaped as lion paws.

COTTAGE PALACE

Drawing Room of Alexandra Feodorovna

⌐ • ⌐

This exhibition reproduces the interior of Alexandra Feodorovna's drawing room at the Cottage Palace in Alexandria Park.

⌐ 213 ⌐

ALEXANDRIA PARK

1847.

Theodor Gudin (1802–1880).

Oils on wood.

27.9 × 42 cm.

On the lower left, signature: J. Gudin 29 Juin 1847 Alexandria.

Inv. No. PDMP 729-zh.

The picture presents a view in the Alexandria Park at Peterhof.

Items on pages 181–197 are found in the Drawing Room of Alexandra Feodorovna on page 180.

⌐ 214 ⌐

EMPEROR NICHOLAS I

1853.

St. Petersburg, Russia.

Galvanoplastic and Casting Firm of the Duke M. Leuchtenberg.

Norbert Schroedl (1816–1890).

Patinaed bronze.

H. 64 cm.

On the base, author's signature and date: "N. Schrodl f 1853" and
mark: "From the Petersburg Galvanoplastic and Casting Firm."

Inv. No. PDMP 863-sk.

The Emperor is here depicted in the uniform of the
Cavalry Guard Regiment, an elite unit of the Guard,
with a ribbon and sign of the Order of Andrei Pervozvanny, the highest Russian decoration, instituted by
Peter I.

⌐ 215 ⌐

THE MAIDEN LAURENTIA OF TANGERMUNDE

1838.

Berlin, Germany.

Christian-Daniel Rauch (1777–1857).

Casting and chasing: Fisher August (1805–1866).

Patinaed bronze, incrustation with colored stones.

H. 45 cm.

On the base, inscription in Latin: "Laurentia virgo Tangermundiana."

Inv. No. PDMP 880-sk.

A subject from medieval Germanic legend: a girl, Laurentia, from the city of Tangermunde, having lost her
way in a wooded thicket, is carried home by a deer.

— 216 —

ITALIAN GENRE PAINTING

1835.

Timothy Neff (1805–1876).

Oil on canvas.

61.6 × 49.5 cm.

On the lower left, signature and date: Nef 1835.

Inv. No. PDMP 747-zh.

— 217 —

ITALIAN WOMAN

1842.

Pimen Orlov (1812–1863).

Oil on canvas.

On the lower right, signature and date: Orlov Roma 1842.

70 × 58 cm.

Inv. No. PDMP 917-zh.

— 218 —

THE EMPRESS ALEXANDRA FEODOROVNA
ON A HORSE

1838.

Model, 1836.

Berlin, Germany.

Gustav Blaeser (1813–1874).

Chasing: Albert Konarzewski.

Patinaed bronze.

H. 50 cm.

Inscription on the base: "Alexandra Feodorowna Keiserin von
Russland Kalisch 1835" and signatures: G. Blaeser fec. Cisel.v.A.
Konarzewski."

Inv. No. PDMP 881-sk.

This equestrian statuette depicts the Empress Alexandra Feodorovna at the large-scale joint maneuvers held by Russian and Prussian troops from August to September 1835 near the city of Kalisz (Poland).

(Photo not available.)

— 219 —

CHANDELIER

1829–1830.

Russia.

Gilded bronze.

H. 61 cm.

Inv. No. PDMP 787-mt

In gothic style, for twelve candles.

— 220 —

MANTLEPIECE CLOCK
"PERFORMING TROUBADOUR"

1828–1829.

Paris, France.

Gilded bronze.

H. 49 cm.

Inv. No. PDMP 223-mt.

In the shape of a gothic arch at the foot of which is a figure of a troubadour playing music.

— 221 —

MANTLEPIECE CLOCK

1828–1829.

Paris, France.

Gilded bronze.

H. 51 cm.

Inv. No. PDMP 240-mt.

In the shape of a gothic arch under which is a seated figure of a woman with a flower in her hand.

— 222 —

CANDLESTICK

1830s.

Russia.

Gilded bronze.

H. 14.6 cm.

Inv. No. PDMP 389-mt

For one candle, shaped as a baluster, on three paw-legs.

— 223 —

FOUR CANDLESTICKS

1820s.

Russia.

Gilded bronze.

H. 33.3 and 30.4 cm.

Inv. No.s PDMP 1745, 1746, 2075, 2076-mt.

In the shape of a column on a round base; candle-holder in the shape of a vase.

— 224 —

LITTLE BELL

1840s.

Russia.

Gilded bronze.

H. 9.5 cm.

Inv. No. PDMP 204-mb.

With a relief depiction of a deer hunt with hounds; handle in the form of a fantastic monster.

～ 225 ～
LITTLE BELL
1830–1840.

Russia.

Bronze, walnut, gilding.

H. 19.2 cm.

Inv. No. PDMP 225-mt

In the form of a bell with a carved handle fashioned as a spire.

～ 226 ～
EMBROIDERY TABLE
1820–1830.

Russia.

Red wood, veneering, carving.

H. 79.5 cm.

Inv. No. PDMP 825-mb.

Octagonal tabletop; the base has one sliding surface with a pincushion on hinges.

An item of furniture that became widespread in connection with the coming into fashion among high society ladies of doing their own embroidery.

～ 227 ～
ARMCHAIR
1820–1830.

Germany.

According to a drawing by K. F. Schinkel (1781–1841).

Walnut, carving.

H. 163 cm.

Inv. No. PDMP 829-mb

A high lancet back with cutout gothic-style ornament, supports for the chair back becoming armrests and with front legs in the form of bundled columns.

～ 228 ～
ARMCHAIR
1830–1840.

Russia.

Red wood, veneering, carving.

H. 96 cm.

Inv. No. PDMP 932-mb.

A deep armchair for resting in. In the 19th century similar armchairs were called "Peaceful." Adorned with carved details in gothic style; legs on wheels, which made it easier to move such a massive article of furniture.

～ 229 ～
SCREEN
1820–1830.

Russia.

Walnut, veneering, carving, colored glass.

H. 130 cm.

Inv. No. PDMP 982-mb

Four-paneled; decorated with colored glass, after medieval stained glass.

Articles of this sort were indispensable in the furnishing of drawing rooms of the first half of the nineteenth century, as they allowed for the creation of several isolated areas for different activities in one interior space.

～ 230 ～
TABLE
1820–1830.

Russia.

Red wood, veneering, carving.

H. 80 cm.

Inv. No. PDMP 1133-mb

Tabletop equipped with a special mechanism allowing it to be brought into a vertical position. This allowed for the table to be used not only for its usual purpose but also as a small decorative screen.

— 231 —
SIX CHAIRS
1820–1830.
Russia.
Red wood, veneering, carving.
H. 92 cm.
Inv. No. PDMP 1140-1145-mb

Rectangular backs, decorated with cutout gothic style ornament.

— 232 —
TWO ETAGERES
Russia.
Walnut, carving.
H. 171 cm.
Inv. No. PDMP 1239-mb. 1820-1830.
Inv. No. PDMP 1731-mb. (reconstructed in imitation of an analogue).

With five shelves, fastened on posts with brackets decorated with cutout gothic-style ornament.
These were used along with display cabinets for displaying the many memorabilia brought from distant travels as souvenirs.

— 233 —
DISPLAY CABINET
1820–1830.
Russia.
Walnut, veneering, carving.
H. 144 cm.
Inv. No. PDMP 1242-mb.

With an open window and five shelves; decorated with applied gothic-style carvings; with a mirrored back wall.

— 234 —
RUG
1850–1860.
Russia.
Canvas, wool yarn, embroidery.
560 × 305 cm.
Inv. No. PDMP 881-tk

The rug is cross-stitched over the entire ground with plant ornament.
Cross-stitched pillows, tablecloths, and rugs were an indispensable part of the decoration of 19th century interiors. Ornament depicting branches with bright multicolored roses was particularly loved.

— 235 —
RUG
Second half of the 19th century.
Russia.
Canvas, wool yarn, embroidery.
220 × 175 cm.
Inv. No. PDMP 891-tk

The rug is cross-stitched over the entire ground with plant ornament.

— 236 —
TABLECLOTH
Second half of the 19th century.
Russia.
Wool, gold thread, weaving.
197.5 × 168 cm.
Inv. No. PDMP 1633-tk

Tapestry tablecloth with flower ornament, edged in fringe.

~ 237 ~

TWIN SCENT VASES WITH LIDS

Russia.

Porcelain, multicolored painting over glaze, gilding.

H. 15.4 cm.

Inv. No. PDMP 1259, 1260-f.

Four-faceted, on legs fashioned as paws. On the front facet, a depiction of a Scottish shepherd with bagpipes (on one vase) and shepherdesses (on the other). On the remaining facets, bouquets of flowers.

~ 238 ~

PAIR OF BUSTS OF CHILDREN

Second quarter of the 19th century.

Model c. 1760.

Meissen, Germany.

Queen's Porcelain Works.

Model by Johann Jaochim Kandler (1706–1775).

Porcelain, multicolored painting over glaze, gilding.

H. 22.5 cm.

Blue marks on unglazed surface: crossed swords.

Inv. No. PDMP 1262, 1263-f.

Depicted are the Princess Maria-Zefirina Bourbon (1750–1755) and her brother the Prince Louis-Charles Bourbon (1751–1761), children of the French Dauphin Louis and his wife, the Saxon Princess Maria-Josefa.

~ 239 ~

CACHE-POT

1825–1830.

Petersburg, Russia.

Imperial Porcelain Factory.

Porcelain, multicolored painting over glaze, gilding.

H. 18.5 cm.

Blue mark over glaze: N I under a crown.

Inv. No. PDMP 1305-f

On each of two sides, a composition of a vase, plant tendrils, flower garlands and birds.

~ 240 ~

BUST OF THE CROWN PRINCESS LUISA

c. 1797.

Berlin, Germany.

Royal Porcelain Works.

Model by Gottfried Schadow (1764–1850).

Biscuit (unglazed pottery).

H. 25.5 cm.

Inv. No. PDMP 3137-f.

The Crown Princess Luisa (1776–1810), spouse of the Prince of Prussia (from 1797, King of Prussia Friedrich-Wilhelm III); mother of the Russian Empress Alexandra Feodorovna, the wife of the Emperor Nicholas I.

— 241 —

SET OF THREE VASES

Second quarter of the 19th century.

Petersburg, Russia.

Imperial Glass Factory.

Cobalt glass, painting in gold.

H. 33.5; 26; 26 cm.

Inv. No. PDMP 553, 554, 556-st.

Blue, with gold painting; the vases are segmented: the large vase consists of three parts; the small ones of two parts.

— 242 —

DECANTER WITH CORK IN A SETTING OF GILDED BRONZE

Second quarter of the 19th century.

Petersburg, Russia.

Imperial Glass Factory.

Milk glass; gilded bronze.

H. 25 cm.

Inv. No. PDMP 797-st.

— 243 —

MUG WITH LID

Second quarter of the 19th century.

Bohemia.

Colorless glass with yellow applied color, etching, engraving.

H. 18.5 cm.

Inv. No. PDMP 805-st

With a depiction of a resort with a healing spring and a colonnade for promenading.

— 244 —

TUMBLER

1820–1830.

Petersburg, Russia.

Imperial Glass Factory.

Faceted crystal, etching, engraving.

H. 14.5 cm.

Inv. No. PDMP 818-st.

On one side, a depiction of the coat of arms of the "Alexandria" dacha; on the other, a deer fleeing from attacking wolves.

— 245 —

TUMBLER

Second quarter of the 19th century.

Bohemia.

Faceted crystal, etching, engraving.

H. 12.8 cm.

Inv. No. PDMP 819-st.

With a depiction of an oriental scene.

— 246 —

SMALL TWIN VASES

1820–1830.

Petersburg, Russia.

Imperial Glass Factory.

Violet crystal, faceted; gilded and patinaed bronze.

H. 19 cm.

Inv. No. PDMP 821/1, 2; 822/1, 2-st.

Shallow vessel of violet crystal resting on a bronze stand with gothic ornament.

— 247 —

TWO TRAYS FOR JEWELRY

Second quarter of the 19th century.

Petersburg, Russia.

Imperial Glass Factory.

Ruby crystal; gilded bronze.

L. 29.7 cm.

Inv. No. PDMP 824, 825-st.

Of oval shape.

~ 248 ~

TWIN VASES

Early 19th century.

Petersburg, Russia.

Imperial Glass Factory.

Ruby crystal; gilded bronze.

H. 16.5 cm.

Inv. No. PDMP 536, 537-st.

The leg of the vase is wound around with the gilded bronze figure of a snake which, raising up, forms a handle.

~ 249 ~

CHEST

Second quarter of the 19th century.

Petersburg, Russia.

Imperial Glass Factory.

Opal glass, painting in gold; gilded bronze.

H. 10 cm.

Inv. No. PDMP 833-st.

In the form of a little trunk.

~ 250 ~

TWIN VASES

Second quarter of the 19th century.

Petersburg, Russia.

Imperial Glass Factory.

Faceted colorless glass with green overlaid color, painting in gold.

H. 16 cm.

Inv. No. PDMP 840, 841-st.

~ 251 ~

PERFUME BOTTLE

c. 1830.

Northern Bohemia.

Cut crystal; gilded bronze; wood; mother-of-pearl; velvet.

H. 13 cm.

Inv. No. PDMP 1015/1, 2-st.

The crystal perfume bottle, shaped as a crown with a gilded bronze setting, lies on a velvet pillow of raspberry color; under the pillow is a low stand with a sliding drawer; the stand is made of wood, finished with thin sheets of mother-of-pearl, and stands on bronze legs fashioned as paws.

~ 252 ~

TWO GLASSES, TWO CANDLESTICKS, AND A RINSE BOWL WITH SAUCER

Second quarter of the 19th century.

Petersburg, Russia.

Imperial Glass Factory.

Blue cloudy glass, faceting.

H. of glasses: 14.3 cm.; of candlesticks: 19.5 cm.; of finger bowl with saucer: 16 cm.

Inv. No. PDMP 1033-1036, 1330/1, 2-st

~ 253 ~

VASE

1820–1830.

Petersburg, Russia.

Imperial Glass Factory.

Ruby and colorless glass, faceting, etching, painting in gold.

H. 21.3 cm.

Inv. No. PDMP 1999-st

In the form of a dolphin supporting a cup.

⟵ 254 ⟶

GLASS

c. 1830s.

Bohemia.

Emanuel Hoffman.

Colorless glass with applied color.

H. 15.3 cm.

Inv. No. PDMP 2352-st.

With an equestrian portrait of the Prussian King Friedrich-Wilhelm III.

⟵ 255 ⟶

CHEST

1830.

Russia.

Rosewood, bronze, watercolor, velvet.

H. 15.5 cm.

Inv. No. PDMP 9-bk

Rosewood box with bronze applique; on the lid, a watercolor of a lady and a gentleman.

⟵ 256 ⟶

STAND WITH MEDALLION

1830.

Russia.

Porcelain, palm and amaranth wood.

H. of stand: 37.8 cm.

Inv. No. PDMP 170-bk, 170/1, 2-bk

Porcelain medallion with a depiction of the Madonna and Child; copy from the painting "Madonna in an Armchair" by Rafael Santi. In a carved frame of palm-wood, and on an ornamented stand made of ama-ranth wood.

⟵ 257 ⟶

LITTLE BASKET

Mid-19th century.

Venice, Italy

Bronze, mosaic.

H. 6.3 cm.

Inv. No. PDMP 200-bk.

This little basket is a souvenir, with mosaic medallions of colored stones, a depiction of flowers, and the in-scription "VENEZIA" in the central medallion.

⟵ 258 ⟶

CHEST

1830s.

Italy.

Copper, marble, lapis lazuli.

H. 8.2 cm.

Inv. No. PDMP 233-bk.

Chest faced with lapis lazuli; on the lid, a medallion of black marble with a mosaic inset.

Aivazovsky

Ivan Konstantinovich AIVAZOVSKY (1817–1900), seascape artist. In 1833–1837, Aivazovsky studied at the Petersburg Academy of Arts as a student of M. Vorobiev and French seascape artist Philipp Tanneur. From 1845 on he was an Academician, from 1847, a professor, and from 1887, an honored member of the Academy of Arts. He traveled widely: in 1840 he visited Italy, Germany, France, England, and Spain. By the 1840s he had already won worldwide recognition. In 1857, at the Paris Exhibition, Aivazovsky received the Order of the Legion of Honor. After the exhibition, in Florence, his self-portrait was installed in the Uffizi Gallery. In 1876 he participated in an exhibition in Philadelphia and won a medal. In 1892 he visited America.

Aivazovsky's paintings became part of the Cottage Palace painting collection after being specially acquired from the artist for that dacha by the Emperor Nicholas I. A number of the canvases were given to Alexandra Feodorovna, the proprietor of the palace, as presents.

— 259 —

SEASCAPE LIT BY THE SETTING SUN. CRIMEA

1842–1843.

I. Aivazovsky.

Oil on canvas.

58 × 88 cm.

On the lower left, signature: Aivazovsky.

Inv. No. PDMP 941-zh.

~ 260 ~

ORIENTAL SCENE

1846.

I. Aivazovsky.

Oil on canvas.

45.5 × 36.5 cm.

On the lower right, signature and date: Aivazovsky 1846.

Inv. No. PDMP 944-zh

~ **261** ~

ORIENTAL SCENE

1846.

I. Aivazovsky.

Oil on canvas.

45.5 × 37 cm.

On the lower left, signature and date: Aivazovsky 1846.

Inv. No. PDMP 945-zh

— 262 —

THE PETERSBURG EXCHANGE

1847.

I. Aivazovsky.

Oil on canvas.

81 × 115 cm.

On the lower right, signature and date: Aivazovsky 1847.

Inv. No. PDMP 942-zh

— 263 —

POTSDAM TROPHY CUP

1830.

Berlin, Germany.

Author of design: Karl-Friedrich Schinkel (1781–1841).

Jeweler: Johann Georg Hossauer (1794–1874).

Silver, chasing, carving, enamel, painting.

H. 75.7 cm.

Marks: on the leg and base, signature: "Georg Hossauer Orfevre du Roi a Berlin 1830."

Inv. No. PDMP 20/1-4-dm.

Decorated with painted enamel coats of arms of noble families of Germany; lid crowned by a rose.

The so-called Potsdam Trophy occupied a central place in the interior of Alexandra Feodorovna's drawing room. It was created to commemorate the famous mock-knightly Tournament of the White Rose, which took place in a Potsdam park, Sans Souci, in July 1829. The festival of the White Rose was celebrated in honor of the Russian Empress; its primary feature was that the invited guests, wearing knightly armor, participated in a special tournament. White roses were the prize for a successfully thrown javelin or an accurate strike of the sword. The cup was commissioned by the father of Alexandra Feodorovna, the Prussian King Friedrich Wilhelm III, from Court Jeweler J. G. Hossauer. The principal adornments of the trophy were the enameled coats of arms of the various participants in the tournament.

TRAIN CAR OF THE TSAR
Abdication of Nicholas II

— · —

Built in 1894, shortly after the 1888 crash of the Tsar's train, in which the family of Alexander III, the father of the future Nicholas II, was traveling. The entire train, with the exception of the Tsar's car, was destroyed. This event was interpreted as a "miracle," but, according to the testimony of experts, the lead bottom of the Tsar's car prevented the walls from collapsing. The new imperial train was supposed to ensure at least the same degree of safety. Its separate parts were constructed in Russia, Germany, France, and Austro-Hungary. During peacetime the train consisted of eleven cars. They included a salon-dining car, a sleeping car, and a nursery, as well as cars for the Grand Princes, for the Tsar's retinue, a staff car, a kitchen car, a workshop, a baggage car, and a wagon for servants. A church car was added later.

In 1929, two cars, with fully preserved appointments and furnishings, were transferred to the Peterhof museum: the sleeping car, which included Alexandra Feodorovna's sleeping quarters, Nicholas II's study, a compartment for a lady's maid and one for a valet; and a dining car. The latter, during wartime, functioned as a headquarters for military conferences; and it was here that, on March 2nd, 1917, Nicholas signed the document abdicating from the Throne of Russia, a document by virtue of which he abdicated not only in his own name but in the name of his son, the Tsarevich Alexei, as well. In this same car, the last Russian Emperor was arrested by representatives of the new government and brought to his family at Tsarskoe Selo. Until the beginning of the Second World War, the car was a museum.

— 264 —

NICHOLAS II'S INKPOT

1903.

London, England.

J. C. Victory

Silver, crystal, faceting, leather; cardboard, leather.

5.5 × 7.7 × 7.7 cm.

Marks: "J. C. V.", a walking lion, a leopard's head, "h", "1001", "14 J. C. VICKERY TO THE QUEEN 181 & 183 REGENT ST W".

Inv. No. PDMP 502, 503-dm.

Crystal, with a low neck appointed in silver and with a silver lid; on the lid, inscription: "Old Nick fr Fared 1903"; in a leather case.

Was kept in the Drawing Room of the Tsar's train, where, according to monarchist V. Shulgin, Nicholas signed his Abdication from the Throne on March 2nd, 1917.

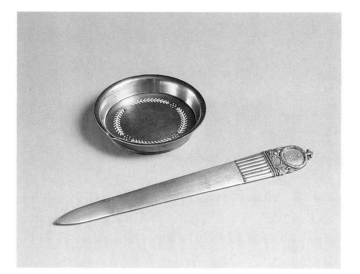

— 265 —

NICHOLAS II'S ASHTRAY IN A CASE

1914.

Moscow, Russia.

K. Fabergé Co.

Silver, relief enamel.

D. 9.1 cm.

Marks: "K. FABERGÉ" under the coat of arms of Russia, and "88"; on the cover of the case, a stamp: "K. FABERGÉ MOSCOW ST. PETERSBURG ODESSA" under the coat of arms of Russia; on the bottom, an inscription in pencil: "For the train December 6th 1914".

Inv. No. PDMP 27, 27/1-dm.

Round, with a flanged edge indented for resting a cigarette; in a grey leathern fabric case.

From the study of Nicholas II in his car of the Tsar's train.

— 266 —

PAPER KNIFE IN A CASE

1915.

Moscow, Russia.

K. Fabergé Co.

Silver, chasing.

L. 20.7 cm. (knife); 23.5 cm. (case).

Marks: on the blade: "K. FABERGÉ", coat of arms of Russia, "84"; on the lid of the case, a stamp: "FABERGÉ PETROGRAD MOSCOW LONDON" under the coat of arms of Russia.

Inv. No. PDMP 64, 64/1-dm

From the study of Nicholas II in his car of the Tsar's train.

— 267 —

ICON: "ALEXANDER NEVSKY"

1899–1903.

Petersburg, Russia.

End of 19th century (painting).

"I. E. Morozov" Co. (1849–1917).

Craftsman's monogram: "SG".

Oils on wood; silver, chasing, gilding,
multicolored enamel on filigree, velvet.

31 × 26.5 cm.

Marks: "SG", "84" on the case: "purveyor to the Court of HIS
IMPER. MAJESTY I. E. MOROZOV ST. PETERSBURG".

Inv. No. PDMP 289, 1002-dm

A depiction of Alexander Nevsky standing; with a silver setting; halo and appliques in the corners of the
setting decorated in multicolored enamel; in an oak
icon case-stand.

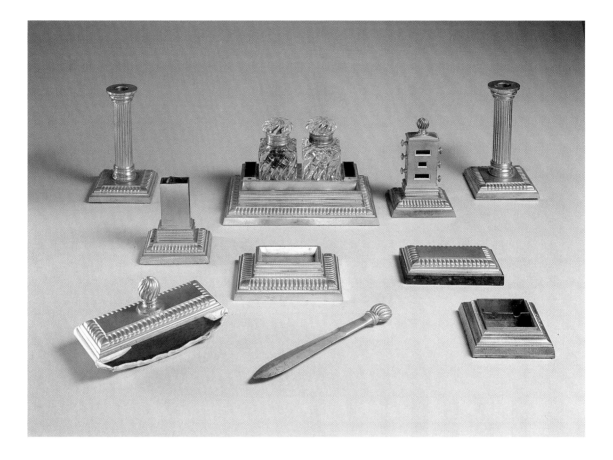

— 268 —

WRITING ENSEMBLE
CONSISTING OF 12 ITEMS:
INKPOT STAND, TWO INKPOTS, PAPER PRESS,
CALENDAR, PAPER WEIGHT, PAPERKNIFE,
ASHTRAY, MATCHBOX, SAND BOX, TWO
CANDLESTICKS. 1890–1900.

Russia.

Gilded bronze, glass, marble, wood, broadcloth.

H. of stand: 4.5 cm.; ink pots: 9.4 cm.; paper press: 8.3 cm.;
calendar: 14.2 cm.; press: 2.5 cm.; knife: 21 cm.; ashtray: 2.5 cm.;
matchbox: 10.3 cm.; sand box: 3.5 cm.; candlesticks: 17 cm.

Inv. No.s PDMP 379-388, 391, 392-mt

Writing ensemble was kept in the study of a car of the
imperial train.

— 269 —

FIVE VASES

Early 20th century.

Village of Kuznetsovo, Tver province, Russia.

Porcelain, green glaze.

H. 12.5 cm., 9 cm., 9 cm., 16 cm., 19 cm.

Inv. No. PDMP 1638, 1640-1643-f.

— 270 —

CLOCK

Second half of 19th century.

Wood, enameled brass, and bronze.

From the saloon-car of the royal train
(the saloon compartment)

H. 34 cm.

Inv. No. PDMP 159-mt.

— 271 —

VASE

1906.

Petersburg, Russia.

Imperial Porcelain Factory.

Porcelain, crystal glaze.

H. 24 cm.

Green mark, under glaze: N II under a crown and date: "1906".

Inv. No. PDMP 1639-f.

— 272 —

VASE

1898.

Petersburg, Russia.

Imperial Porcelain Factory.

H. 49.5 cm.

Green mark, under glaze: N II under a crown and date: "1898".

Inv. No. PDMP 5080-f.

PHOTOGRAPHS OF THE ROMANOV FAMILY

— 273 —

FRAME WITH PHOTOGRAPH

1896–1903.

Petersburg, Russia.

Fabergé.

Andres Nevalainen.

Silver, chasing, translucent enamel on a guilloche ground.

20.9 × 15 cm.

Mark: "FABERGÉ", "A. N", "88".

Inv. No. PDMP 664-dm.

Covered in transparent red enamel and adorned with silver wreaths and garlands. Photo: Grand Duchess Maria Feodorovna, wife of Emperor Alexander III and mother of the Emperor Nicholas II.

Heir to the Throne Tsarevich Alexei Nikolaevich in Russian costume.

Also on display:

- Empress Alexandra Feodorovna (wife of Emperor Nicholas II).

- Heir to the Throne Tsarevich Alexei Nikolaevich (son of Emperor Nicholas II), saluting.

- Heir to the Throne Tsarevich Alexei Nikolaevich in an armchair on the terrace, in military uniform.

- Grand Duchess Olga Nikolaevna (daughter of Emperor Nicholas II).

- Grand Duchess Tatiana Nikolaevna (daughter of Emperor Nicholas II).

- Grand Duchess Ksenia Alexandrovna (daughter of Emperor Alexander III, sister of Emperor Nicholas II) on a swing.

The Yellow Hall

DINING WITH THE TSARS

—•—

The Peterhof residence was a place where, during the summertime, there was a constant series of celebrations, festivals, and fireworks. These became particularly opulent and attractive in the 19th century. Throughout the century, dinners were the central ritual of official celebrations. Dining was an extraordinarily conservative ritual that was not altered until the end of the reign of the House of Romanov. A dinner given in honor of one or another guest of high status called for the arrangement of a U-shaped head table where a place for the Emperor was designated. For guests of less exalted levels, separate round or oval tables were set. Receptions were usually intended for a wide circle of invited guests: ladies in waiting of the Court, high ranking merchants, military men, clergy, etc., and places at the tables were strictly assigned.

Regimental celebrations were often held at Peterhof; for these, tables were set for over three thousand people. For these, tables were arranged throughout the entire suite of ceremonial halls, in the lower level galleries, and even simply in the park. This all required enormous auxiliary rooms, a large number of cooks and serving personnel, and vast quantities of dishware. During such celebrations at Peterhof, many services of more than a hundred place settings would be used, and in each room of the palace, tables were set with a different kind of dishes.

A menu would be laid at each place setting. This custom was strictly observed, at receptions of the very highest rank as well as at purely internal Peterhof celebrations, whether Peter's Day, the name-day of Maria Feodorovna, or, perhaps, Alexandra Feodorovna's birthday. Many people took these menu cards home with them, accumulating entire collections of such souvenirs of festive dinners at the Imperial Palaces.

The Peterhof Collection has preserved some of these menu cards. Here, for example, is the menu for a dinner given in honor of the King of Siam, Chulalankorn, at the Great Palace at Peterhof:

> *DINER*
> *du 22 Juin 1897.*
> *Potages: Mignon, Tortue Clair*
> *Petits pates*
> *Sterlet au vin de l'Ermitage*
> *Selle de Chevreuil d'Allemagne S-ce Venaison*
> *Noisettes de Faisans a la Clamart*
> *Foie de Canard aux Truffes du Perigord*
> *Sorbets*
> *Pulardes de la Fleche roties*
> *Salade*
> *Asperges en branches S-ce Mousseuse*
> *Peches de Montreuil a la Royale*
> *Madeleine glacee*
> *Dessert.*

And here is the recipe for "Soup with Rice and Salmon, Peterhof style:"

Prepare a stock: take two chickens roasted on a rotisserie, a little beef, and the required amount of water; skim off the foam, add two carrots, two turnips, two onions and a bunch of leeks. After boiling for five minutes, remove the fat from the stock, clarify it, and pour one quarter of the stock into a pot into which you have placed six ounces of washed and blanched Carolina rice. Cut two carrots, add small scallops of perch and eel, saute and salt them. Let it boil for ten minutes and remove the sediment. Then pour the stock into a soup tureen into which you have put the rice as well as salmon, goose liver, and a half-liter of green peas prepared English style. Serve.

Both dinner and tea services used in the Imperial palaces are presented in the section "Russian Table."

— 274 —

TAPESTRY "PETER THE FIRST
IN A STORM ON LAKE LADOGA"

1814–1818.

Paris, France.

Queen's Tapestry Factory.

After a painting by Charl von Steuben (1788–1856).

Wool, silk, 8 threads per cm.

390 × 350 cm.

On the right corner, woven signature: STEUBEN.

Inv. No. PDMP 277-tk.

The subject of the tapestry "Peter the Great in a Storm on Lake Ladoga" was inspired by actual events.

On the tapestry the Emperor Peter I (the Great) is shown dressed in the uniform of an officer of the Semyonovsky Regiment, and wearing an Order of Andrei Pervozvanny, the highest decoration in Russia, which was bestowed on him for taking prisoner a Swedish ship. The Tsar is fearlessly guiding his perishing vessel through the raging waves, a model of personal courage for his despairing oarsmen.

Woven at the Gobelin Tapestry Works by order of Napoleon I as a present for Russian Emperor Alexander I; designed after a painting by S. Steuben. The painting, exhibited in 1812 at the Paris Salon, was enthusiastically received; it was acquired by Napoleon I and later reproduced not only in tapestry form, but in graphic art, sculpture, and embroidery.

Work on this tapestry was begun in June 1814, though in October of that same year, work on it was interrupted, to be renewed only in January 1815. In 1819 the tapestry was completed and presented at the Industrial Exhibition at the Louvre.

The tapestry was delivered to the Emperor Alexander I through the Ministry of Foreign Affairs, and arrived at the Winter Palace in November 1820. In 1820 it arrived at Peterhof.

At the present time the tapestry is installed in the Yellow Hall of the Catherine Wing, where the famous Russian Service (Cat. No. 290) is also on display.

275

MENU OF A STATE DINNER IN HONOR
OF THE ENGAGEMENT
OF GRAND DUKE NICHOLAS NIKOLAEVICH
TO ALEXANDRA PETROVNA
OF OLDENBURG

1855.

Petersburg, Russia.

Lithograph by A. Petersen.

Drawing by Peter von Hess (1792–1871).

Paper, color lithography.

29.3 × 20.2 cm.

Inv. No. PDMP 23-pg.

This is one of the earliest examples of the genre of Russian artist's menus, which first appeared in the middle of the last century, replacing hand-written menus. The menu's decorative border is crowned by two coats of arms: the Russian and that of the Oldenburg dukedom.

Grand Duke Nicholas Nikolaevich, the third son of the Emperor Nicholas I, was married to Alexandra Petrovna (Friederika-Wilhelmina), Princess of Oldenburg. The betrothal ceremony and ceremonial dinner honoring it took place on November 13th, 1855, at the Nikolaevsky Palace in Petersburg. During the summertime, the Grand Duke's family lived at the country estate of Znamenka, not far from the Peterhof ceremonial residence, given to the Grand Duke by his father.

DINER
7 Mai 1884.

Potages: Bisque de Homards.
Consommé aux laitues farcies
Petits pâtés divers
Poisson: Truites saumonées à la Chambord
Relevé de boucherie: Pièces de boeuf à la
Flamande
Entrées: Petites caisses de mauviettes à la
Perigueux
Filets de Dindes à la gelée
Punch Royal
Roti: Cannetons de Rouen, Doubles et Bécasses
Salade
Légumes: Asperges en branches,
Sauce Hollandaise
Entremet sucré: Crème bavaroise aux fraises
Glaces
Dessert.

— 276 —

MENU OF A STATE DINNER GIVEN ON MAY 7TH, 1884, IN HONOR
OF THE SIXTEENTH BIRTHDAY OF THE HEIR TO THE THRONE
GRAND DUKE NICHOLAS ALEXANDROVICH

1884.

Petersburg, Russia.

Lithograph by A. Ilyin.

Drawing by Lev Feliksovich Lagorio (1827–1905).

Cardboard, color lithography.

40.2 × 26 cm.

Inv. No. PDMP 30-pg.

On May 6, 1884, the Heir to the Throne, Tsarevich Grand Duke Nicholas Alexandrovich, the future Emperor Nicholas II, turned 16. An official dinner was held on the day following his formal oath-taking at the Nikolaevsky Hall of the Winter Palace. On the menu, in a decorative border, under crowns, were the monograms of the Emperor Alexander III and the Empress Maria Feodorovna, the parents of Nicholas, as well as the Heir's own monogram.

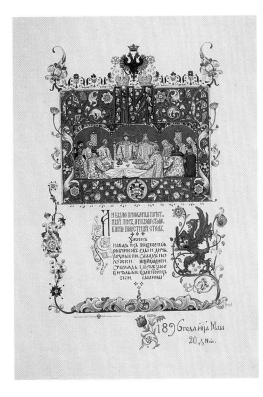

— 277 —

MENU OF A STATE SUPPER IN HONOR OF THE
CORONATION OF THE EMPEROR NICHOLAS II
AND THE EMPRESS ALEXANDRA FEODOROVNA

1896.

Moscow, Russia.

A. A. Levenson Press.

Drawing by Viktor Mikhailovich Vasnetsov (1848–1926).

Paper, color lithography.

43.5 × 31 cm.

Inv. No. PDMP 27-pg.

The seventh day of the coronation festivities ended
with a ball given at the residence of the General-Gov-
ernor of Moscow, Grand Duke Sergei Alexandrovich.
When Their Highnesses arrived, the dancing began,
accompanied by the sounds of the string orchestra of
the Preobrazhensky Royal Guard Regiment. At one
o'clock in the morning, a supper for 1,500 was served.
Before each plate was placed an elegantly printed
menu executed after a drawing by artist V. Vasnetsov, a depiction of an Old Russian Tsar's feast and
the Romanov coat of arms.

— 278 —

MENU OF A STATE DINNER AND PROGRAM OF A
CONCERT HELD IN HONOR OF THE 300-YEAR
ANNIVERSARY OF THE HOUSE OF ROMANOV

1913.

Petersburg, Russia.

Printed by S. M. Proskudin-Gorsky.

Drawing by Ivan Yakovlevich Bilibin (1876–1942).

Paper, color lithography.

43.4 × 16.2 cm.

Inv. No. PDMP 44-pg.

On February 21st, 1913, celebration of the three-hundred-year anniversary of the reign of the House of Romanov began in Petersburg. The final day of celebrations was marked by a state dinner for 1100 invited guests, held in four halls of the Winter Palace: the St. George Hall, the Coat of Arms Hall, the Alexander Hall, and the Military Gallery. In the St. George Hall, where a royal table was placed for the Emperor, the orchestra of the Preobrazhensky Royal Guard Regiment played. During the toasts, cannons were fired from Peter and Paul Fortress.

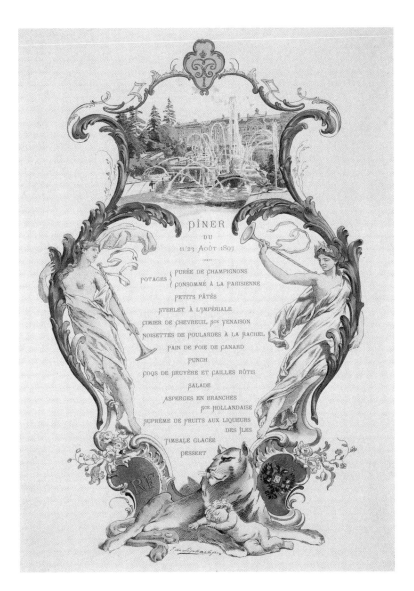

— 279 —

MENU OF A STATE DINNER AT THE GREAT
PALACE AT PETERHOF, GIVEN IN HONOR
OF A VISIT BY FRENCH PRESIDENT F. FAURE

1897.

Petersburg, Russia.

Drawing by Ernest Karlovich Liepgart (1847–1932).

Cardboard, color lithography.

34.5 × 24.9 cm.

Inv. No. PDMP 46-pg.

For this state dinner, tables were set for 200 people with the Guriev Service (Cat. No. 290), in two halls of the palace: the Throne Hall, where the Imperial table was located, and the Merchant Hall. As to all such celebrations, all of the Grand Dukes and Duchesses, the President's retinue, ranking officers of the French Embassy and their spouses, ministers, and the highest retinue of the Tsar were invited. Along the sides of the hall, from the doors, in garb richly embroidered with gold—velvet jackets, wide red trousers, and small hats—stood the Court Blackamoors (Cat. No. 287).

According to the rules of Court etiquette, the central place at table belonged to the Empress; the Tsar was to be on her left, and the President on her right; the Grand Dukes and Duchesses were seated on both sides. At each table setting was laid a menu where, in a festive border of flowers, cupids, and stylized ornament, under the coat of arms of the Peterhof ceremonial residence, there was a picture of the Great Palace. Allegorical figures along the edges symbolized the themes of music and celebration. The musical program was performed by the Court Orchestra, which began its program with the overture from M. Glinka's "Life for the Tsar".

~ 280 ~

PROGRAM OF A STATE RECEPTION
AT PETERHOF GIVEN IN HONOR OF A VISIT
BY THE SHAH OF PERSIA

1900.

Moscow, Russia.

A. A. Levenson Press.

Paper, color lithography.

25.8 × 49.8 cm.

Inv. No. PDMP 49-pg.

A state dinner on the occasion of a visit to Peterhof by
the Persian Shah Muzafer-Eddin was held in the
Great Palace at Peterhof. Tables were set for 188 people in the Throne and Merchant Halls. Royalty was
served at table by chamber pages. During dinner, the
Court Orchestra played in the Chesmen Hall.

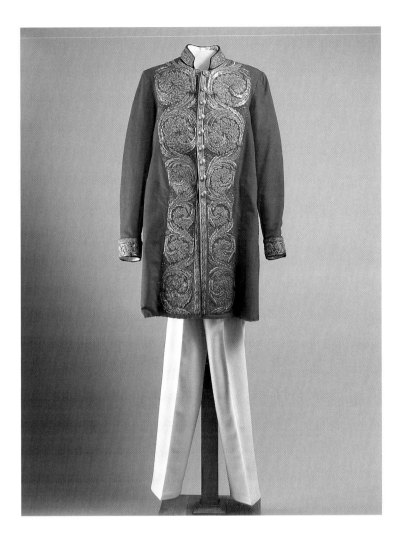

— 281 —

SENATOR'S DRESS UNIFORM

End of 19th–early 20th century.

Russia.

Broadcloth, velvet, gold stitching, gilded bronze.

H. 95 cm.

Inv. No. PDMP 1056, 1610-tk.

The official dress uniform of a Senator, of scarlet broadcloth with uniform gold stitching in the form of stylized oak and laurel branches, and gilded bronze buttons with the inscription "Law". Trousers of white cloth with gold galloon lace. Two-cornered black felt hat with gold galloon lace, cockade and black ostrich feather.

Each ranking Court officer had a specific uniform corresponding to his rank. There were different versions of the uniforms for ball, holiday, and everyday occasions. The higher the position of a given person, the more gold stitching there was on his uniform.

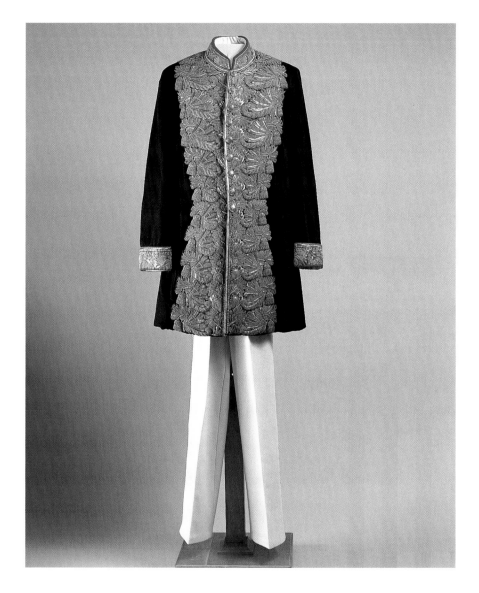

— 282 —

CHAMBERLAIN'S DRESS UNIFORM
End of 19th–early 20th century.
Russia.
Broadcloth, gold stitching, gilded bronze.
H. 91 cm.
Inv. No. PDMP 1057-tk, 2047-mt.

The dress uniform of a Chamberlain, of black broadcloth, uniform gold stitching forming stylized plant and peacock feather ornament, and gilded buttons with a coat of arms. Trousers of white broadcloth with gold galloon lace.

The title of Court Chamberlain was introduced in Russia in the 18th century. Originally, the Chamberlain was a Court official in charge of a branch of Court administration. This accounts for one element of the Chamberlain's regalia, a key on a ribbon.

— 283 —

COURT COSTUME (BODICE, TRAIN,
KOKOSHNIK [RUSSIAN TRADITIONAL
WOMAN'S HEADDRESS], BEADS)

Second half of 19th century.

Russia.

Velvet, silk, silver thread, sequins, artificial pearls.

H. of bodice: 36 cm.
H. of train: 307 cm.
H. of kokoshnik: 10 cm.

Inv. No. PDMP 391-394-tk.

Court dress: bodice, train of apricot-colored velvet
with silver stitching in the form of rich flower ornamentation, white silk skirt. Kokoshnik of apricot-
colored velvet adorned with artificial pearls. Beads of
artificial pearls.

— 284 —

DRESS COSTUME OF THE COURT TUTORESS
TO THE GRAND DUCHESSES (BODICE, SKIRT,
TRAIN, KOKOSHNIK [RUSSIAN TRADITIONAL
WOMAN'S HEADDRESS])

Last half of 19th century.

Russia.

Velvet, silk, gold stitching.

H. of bodice: 33 cm.
H. of skirt: 143 cm.
H. of train: 261 cm.
H. of kokoshnik: 5.5 cm.

Inv. No.s PDMP 387, 486, 388, 389-bk.

The women's Court dress costume was introduced in 1834 by a special decree of Nicholas I, according to which the cut, texture, and color of the fabric and ornamentation used for women's costumes were strictly regulated. The new Court dresses, borrowing certain characteristics of ancient Russian costume, consisted of an open-front outerdress with a train and long folding sleeves, and an underdress of white silk, both decorated with gold and silver stitching. The costume was completed by the traditional Russian woman's headdress, the kokoshnik, with a veil for ladies and a fillet and veil for maidens. The color of the velvet, the character and material of the stitching, and the length of the train were all strictly regulated in accordance with the position occupied in Court by the lady or her husband. Thus, for example, the approved Court dress of the imperial daughters' tutoress had to be made of dark blue velvet and gold stitching of a pattern identical to the stitching of the dress uniforms of highly placed officials of the Court. This kind of Court dress was preserved until 1917, modified only in details. From the mid-19th century it consisted of a corsage bodice, removable train, and a white silk skirt.

— 285 —

DOORMAN'S COSTUME
(JACKET, VEST, TROUSERS)
End of 19th century–early 20th century.

Russia.

Broadcloth, velvet, galloon lace, gilded bronze.

H. of jacket: 101 cm.
H. of vest: 70 cm.
H. of trousers: 106 cm.

Inv. No. PDMP 577, 583, 590-tk.

A jacket of green broadcloth adorned with galloon uniform lace with eagles and gilded buttons with coats of arms. Vest of red broadcloth with gilded galloon and coat of arms buttons. Trousers of blue velvet with brown broadcloth gaiters. Costumes of servants in the imperial palaces, including those of chamber lackeys, hall porters, footmen, gentlemen of the bedchamber, and others, were distinguished by their exceptionally decorative appearance. They were made of fabric of highly saturated colors and were richly adorned by uniform gold galloon lace with depictions of the imperial coat of arms and by gilded buttons with coat of arms.

— 286 —

WAITER'S COSTUME
End of 19th–early 20th century.

Russia.

Broadcloth, velvet, galloon lace, gilded bronze.

H. 108 cm.

Inv. No. PDMP 597-tk.

A swallowtail coat of dark blue broadcloth with collar adorned with gilded galloon lace, with two rows of coat of arms buttons. Blue broadcloth trousers.

— 287 —

COSTUME OF COURT "BLACKAMOOR"
(BAMBET JACKET, WIDE TROUSERS, HAT)

End of 19th–early 20th century.

Russia.

Broadcloth, velvet, galloon lace, gold cord.

H. of bambet (jacket): 60 cm.
H. of trousers: 117 cm.
H. of hat: 17 cm.

Inv. No. PDMP 579, 580, 585-tk.

Bambet jacket and wide trousers of red broadcloth with gold galloon, hat of red velvet with gold cord and tassles. It was a tradition of sorts that important formal receptions and balls at the Imperial palaces were served by, in addition to the court lackeys, dark-skinned servants dressed in exotic "blackamoor" costumes.

— 288 —

TWIN VASES

1810s.

Petersburg, Russia.

Imperial Porcelain Factory.

Porcelain, multicolored painting over glaze, gilding, ornamental cutting, gilded bronze.

H. 55 and 54.5 cm.

Inv. No.s PDMP 7405, 7406-f.

In blank areas, depiction of scenes from the education of Eros by Venus.

⁓ 289 ⁓

PAIR OF VASES

1825–1835.

Petersburg, Russia.

Imperial Porcelain Factory.

Porcelain, monochromatic coating over glaze, gilding,
ornamental cutting, multicolored painting over glaze.

H. 58 cm.

Marks: blue, under glaze: N I under a crown.

Inv. No. PDMP 2793, 2794-f.

On one vase, in an unpainted area, a copy of a painting
by Italian artist Benedetto Luti (1666–1724) "A
Young Musician"; on the other vase, a copy of "Young
Woman's Head in a Bonnet" by French artist Jean-
Baptiste Greuze (1725–1805).

The paintings "A Young Musician" and "Young
Woman's Head in a Bonnet" are among prominent
works of art that are part of the Picture Gallery at the
Imperial Hermitage in Saint Petersburg. Many paintings from this collection were copied by artists at the
Imperial Porcelain Factory on display vases intended
for the decor of imperial palace interiors.

— 290 —

ITEMS FROM THE RUSSIAN "GURIEV" SERVICE

For 18 persons.

Petersburg, Russia.

Imperial Porcelain Factory.

The service was manufactured in 1809–1817. The name "Russian" is used in reference to it in archival documents until 1824. The service's second name, "Guriev," was given when it was named after Count D. Guriev, a minister to the Imperial Court, who supervised the Imperial Porcelain Factory at that time. The service was intended for the Main Palace Administration. The primary concept behind the service's decoration was the celebration of the great size of the Russian Empire. Leading masters of the Imperial Porcelain Factory, painters A. Kanunnikov and S. Shifliar, ornamentalists G. Ziuzin and I. Ankudinov, and the gilder Bokur participated in creating the service. The ground color of the service is red-brown, with gold plant ornament. The unpainted reserves on the items feature multicolored depictions of scenes, the subjects of which were taken from the books "Description of All Peoples Residing in the Russian State" by I. Georgi and "Petersburg Scenes and Types" by C. G. H. Geissler, as well as from views of Petersburg and Moscow copied from works by F. Alexeev, M. Vorobev, S. Shchedrin, and S. Galaktionov. In the second half of the 19th century, compositions by I. Shchedrovsky, from the publication "Scenes from Russian Folk Life," served as sources for the paintings. The gilded, sculptural details of the vases, executed from models by S. Pimenov and I. Komander, play a large role in the decoration of the service. The service includes dinner, dessert, and tea elements. The service was originally intended for 50 people. Under Emperors Nicholas I and Nicholas II the service was augmented by tea and coffee settings and a large lot of dessert plates, and came eventually to include more than 4500 items. In 1848 the service from the Winter Palace was transferred to Peterhof for use at the formal table in the Catherine Wing of Monplaisir during the yearly balls in honor of graduates of the Smolny Institute for Noble Maidens, founded by Catherine the Great. In addition, the service was used more than once to set the tables at the Great Palace at Peterhof for solemn official Imperial receptions for heads of foreign states, for example, the service was used at the reception for the first President of the French Republic to visit Russia, F. Faure, in 1897, and at a reception for the Japanese delegation headed by Prince Katohito Kan-In in 1900.

Items on pages 226–231 are found in The Yellow Hall shown on page 206.

⁓ · ⁓

EIGHTEEN FLAT PLATES

1809–1817.

Porcelain, monochromatic covering over glaze, gilding, ornamental
cutting; multicolored painting over glaze on bottom.

D. 25 cm.

1. With a picture of Sayan Tatars.
   On reverse, black glazed inscription: Tatares Sayans.
      Inv. No. PDMP 1994-f.

2. With a picture of a female resident of the town of Tver.
   On reverse, black inscription over glaze: Femme de Tver /(in
   Russian:) Tver merchant wife Manf re Imper le de Russie
      Inv. No. PDMP 2031-f

3. With a picture of a Black Sea Cossack.
   On reverse, black inscription over glaze: Cosaque de la Mer noire.
      Inv. No. PDMP 3172-f

4. With a picture of an Estonian woman.
   On reverse, black inscription over glaze: (in Russian:)
   Estonian woman; Femme Esthonienne Manf re Imper
   le de Russie
      Inv. No. PDMP 3183-f

5. With a picture of a female cook and a fisherman.
   On reverse, black inscription over glaze: (in Russian:) Cook and
   Fisherman; Le marchand de poisson avec un cuisiniere. Manf
   re Imper le de Russie
      Inv. No. PDMP 3194-f

6. With a picture of a butcher.
   On reverse, black inscription over glaze: Butcher Un Boucher
   Manf re Imper le de Russie
      Inv. No. PDMP 3196-f

7. With a picture of a nut merchant with a female customer.
   On reverse, black inscription over glaze: Le marchand de
   noisettes; (in Russian:) Peddler Manf re Imper le de Russie
   with nuts
      Inv. No. PDMP 3197-f

8. With a picture of residents of the city of Tashkent. (Artist S.
   Shifliar [1785–?]).
   On reverse, black inscription over glaze: (in Russian:) Tashkin
   wench; Femme tachekine. Manf re Imper le de Russie; *along
   the internal rim, signature of the artist:* Chiflar p.
      Inv. No. PDMP 3200-f

9. With a picture of a female Kirghiz sultan.
   On reverse, black inscription over glaze: Sultane Kirguise
      Inv. No. PDMP 3205-f

10. With a picture of a peddler and a peasant.
    On reverse, black inscription over glaze: Paysan en habit de
    voyage et Marchand d'oeufs; (in Russian:) Peasant in traveling
    clothes and peddler Manf re Imper le de Russie
       Inv. No. PDMP 3206-f

11. With a picture of a hawker of Easter eggs with a customer.
    On reverse, black inscription over glaze: (in Russian:) Peddler of
    Easter eggs; Un Marchand d'oeufs de paques Manf re Imper le
    de Russie
       Inv. No. PDMP 2038-f

12. With a picture of female resident of the city of Cherkask.
    On reverse, black inscription over glaze: Femme de la Ville de
    Tcherkask.
       Inv. No. PDMP 2062-f

13. With a picture of a young Valdai woman.
    On reverse, black inscription over glaze: (in Russian:)Valdai
    Peasant Girl; Une Felle de Walday Manf re Imper le de Russie
       Inv. No. PDMP 2032-f

14. With a picture of a peddler with cakes.
    On reverse, black inscription over glaze: (in Russian:) Peddler with
    cakes; Le Marchand de Gateaux Manf re Imper le de Russie
       Inv. No. PDMP 2036-f

15. With a picture of a peddler of greens and a glazier.
    On reverse, black inscription over glaze: Le vitzier et le Marchand
    de legumes; (in Russian:) Peddler of vegetables and glazier
    Manf re Imper le de Russie
       Inv. No. PDMP 2037-f

16. With a picture of Greek woman and man.
    On reverse, black inscription over glaze: Une Greque, et un Grec
       Inv. No. PDMP 2040-f

17. With a picture of a shaman.
    On reverse, black inscription over glaze: Une Chamane
       Inv. No. PDMP 2041-f

18. With a picture of a girl and a woman, residents of the city
    of Bratsk.
    On reverse, black inscription over glaze: Une fille & une femme
    Bratzke
       Inv. No. PDMP 2042-f

— · —

18 FLAT PLATES

1809–1817.

Porcelain, monochromatic covering over glaze,
gilding, ornamental cutting.

D. 25 cm.

Inv. No.s PDMP 1974-1977, 1980, 1982-1985,
1989-1991, 2003-2006, 2109, 3455-f

In the center of plates, a gold rosette.

— · —

18 DEEP PLATES

1809–1817, 1892, 1855–1881, 1898.

Porcelain, monochromatic covering over glaze,
gilding, ornamental cutting.

H. 23.5 cm.

On three plates, green marks under glaze: A III 92, A II,
N II 1898 under a crown.

Inv. No.s PDMP 3240-5811-f

In center of plates, gold rosette.

— · —

6 BOTTLE BUCKETS

1809–1817.

Porcelain, monochromatic covering over glaze, gilding,
ornamental cutting; multicolored painting over glaze
in unpainted areas.

H. 20 cm.

1. In unpainted areas, views of Saint Petersburg: the Palace
Square and the Embankment of the Neva River. After 1834.
   Inv. No. PDMP 1950-f

2. In unpainted areas, views of Saint Petersburg: the Admiralty
and a fragment of the Peter and Paul Fortress.
   Inv. No. PDMP 3157-f

3. In unpainted areas, views of the park at Gatchina: palace from
the side of the Long Island of the White Lake and the Stone
Bridge near Konnetable Square.
   Inv. No. PDMP 3165-f

4. In unpainted areas, views of Saint Petersburg: Monument to
Peter I on the Senate Square and a fragment of the Peter and
Paul Fortress.
   Inv. No. PDMP 3171-f

5. In unpainted areas, views of the park at Pavlovsk and the Marly
Palace in the Lower Park of Peterhof.
   Inv. No. PDMP 3161-f

6. In unpainted areas, views of the Kamennoostrovsky (Stone
Island) Palace in Saint Petersburg. 1815–1817.
   (Porcelain, monochromatic covering over glaze, painting in
   gold, ornamental cutting, monochromatic printed drawing
   over glaze.
   Inv. No. PDMP 1948-f

━ ∙ ━

FRUIT VASE "THE FOUR SEASONS"

1809–1817.

Porcelain, monochromatic covering over glaze, gilding, ornamental cutting.

H. 69 cm.

Inv. No. PDMP 3147-f

The bowl rests on a pedestal with three female figures in Russian costumes.

━ ∙ ━

TWIN FRUIT VASES "VESTAL VIRGINS"

1809–1817.

Porcelain, monochromatic covering over glaze, gilding, ornamental cutting.

H. 46 cm.

Inv. No.s PDMP 1937, 1939-f

The vessel rests on four figures of vestal virgins.

━ ∙ ━

TWIN FRUIT VASES "WOMEN ON THEIR KNEES"

1809–1817.

Porcelain, monochromatic covering over glaze, gilding, ornamental cutting.

H. 36.4 cm.

Inv. No.s PDMP 3367, 3368-f

The vessel rests on a female figure in a sarafan (traditional Russian robe) and kokoshnik (traditional Russian women's headdress).

━ ∙ ━

FOUR ICE CREAM COOLERS

1809–1817.

Porcelain, monochromatic covering over glaze, gilding, ornamental cutting, multicolored painting over glaze.

H. 39 cm.

Inv. No.s PDMP 3321-3323, 3370-f

With a depiction of dancing peasants in Russian garb.

— · —

COMPOTE CHALICE ON A SAUCER

1809−1817. 1892.

Porcelain, monochromatic covering over glaze, gilding, ornamental cutting.

H. of compote dishes: 19.2 cm.; L. of saucer: 18.1 cm.

On one of the compote dishes, a green mark under glaze: N II under a crown and date "92".

Inv. No. PDMP 2134/1, 2; 2136/1, 2; 3285/1, 2-f

Compote dish in the form of a cup supported by a female figure on her knees in Russian costume.

— · —

COMPOTE CHALICE ON A SAUCER

1809−1817. 1899.

Porcelain, monochromatic covering over glaze, gilding, ornamental cutting.

On the two compote dishes, a green mark under glaze: N II under a crown and date] "1899".

Inv. No. PDMP 2151/1, 2; 3280/1, 2; 3372/1, 2-f

In the form of a round bowl resting on the figure of an eagle.

— · —

2 SAUCE BOATS WITH SAUCERS, 2 SAUCE PITCHERS WITH SAUCERS, 18 CREAM POTS AND 9 SALT CELLARS

1809−1817.

Porcelain, monochromatic covering over glaze, gilding, ornamental cutting.

H. of sauce boats: 17.5 cm.; L. of saucers: 30 cm.; H. of sauce pitchers: 19.5; L. of saucers: 28.8 cm.; H. of cream pots: 6.3 cm.; H. of salt cellars: 4.

Inv. No. PDMP 3356/1-3295-f

— · —

TWO SALAD BOWLS

1825−1881.

Porcelain, monochromatic covering over glaze, gilding, ornamental cutting.

H. 10 cm.

Marks: on one bowl, blue, under glaze—N I under a crown, on the other, under glaze—N II under a crown.

Inv. No. PDMP 2200, 2201-f

~ 291 ~

CRYSTAL ITEMS BELONGING
TO THE GURIEV SERVICE

1801.

Ireland. Waterford. 1784–1851.

Together with the "Guriev" ("Russian") service, the table is
set with items from the crystal "Minister" service, ordered at
the end of the 18th century by Emperor Paul I. These items
were manufactured at the Waterford factory in Ireland,
but, insofar as the commission was made through England,
the work has traditionally been called "English." Delivered
to Russia in 1802.

~ · ~

FOUR VASES FOR BERRIES AND BISCUITS
Cut crystal; bronze, chasing, gilding.
H. 19 cm.
Inv. No.s PDMP 996, 1389, 1421, 1447, 1448, 1452-st
Consists of crystal bowls and bronze bases.

~ · ~

2 JAM VASES
Cut crystal.
H. 21 cm.
Inv. No.s PDMP 1438, 1394-st

— • —

2 SUGAR BOWLS

Cut crystal.

H. 24 cm.

Inv. No.s PDMP 1393, 1394-st

— • —

9 SALT CELLARS WITH SAUCERS

Cut crystal.

H. of salt cellars: 5.5 cm.;
diameter of saucers: 11.6 cm.

Inv. No.s PDMP 1000/1, 2-1432/1, 2-st

— • —

6 CARAFES

Cut crystal.

H. 28.5 and 24 cm.

Inv. No.s PDMP 1157, 1383, 1385-1387, 1434-st

— • —

36 WINE GLASSES

Cut crystal.

H. 15.3, 13, 11 cm.

Inv. No.s PDMP 915-918, 964-971, 1397-1418, 1429, 1813-st

— • —

**4 PLATES, 2 BOTTLE BUCKETS,
2 SAUCE BOATS, 2 ICE CREAM COOLERS**

Cut crystal.

D. of plates: 22.5 cm.; H. of bottle buckets: 10.5 cm.;
H. of sauce boats: 9.5 cm.; H. of coolers: 31 cm.

Inv. No.s PDMP 929-931, 940, 921, 923, 991, 992, 1391, 1392-st

— • —

**TWIN VASES TO THE "PRIGOROD"
("COUNTRY") FACETED SERVICE"**

Cut crystal.

H. 27.5 cm.

Inv. No.s PDMP 974, 975-st.

— 292 —

KNIVES AND FORKS

1843.

Zlatoust, Ural Mountains, Russia.

Pavel Anosov (1799–1851), steelwork.

Petersburg, English store "Nikols and Plinke".

Steel, gold inlay, elephant ivory.

L. 23.3 cm. (knives); L. 19.3 cm. (forks).

On blades, engraved: "Zlatoust 1843".

Inv. No.s PDMP 680-709-715 mt (knives); 719-750-753 mt (forks).

For 18 persons. Knife blades of steel with "A I" in gold inlay under an imperial crown; hafts of elephant ivory, faceted. Fork with three tines, matching haft.

The silverware was commissioned by the Emperor Nicholas I to supplement similar pieces prepared in 1818–1825 for Alexander I.

Great Palace Banquet Service

— 293 —

ITEMS FROM THE GREAT PALACE
BANQUET SERVICE

For 12 persons.

12 SOUP BOWLS, 24 FLAT PLATES, 12 OVAL SALT
CELLARS, 12 ROUND SALT CELLARS, 12 POTS
FOR CREAM, 12 ROSETTE DISHES FOR OYSTERS,
4 SAUCE BOATS WITH COVERS AND SAUCERS,
4 SALAD BOWLS, 4 FRUIT VASES

1848–1853.

Petersburg, Russia.

Imperial Porcelain Factory.

Porcelain, multicolored painting over glaze, gilding.

Blue marks under glaze: N I under a crown.

D. of deep dishes: 25 cm.; of flat plates: 24.6 cm.; H. of salt cellars: 4
cm.; of cream pots: 7 cm.; of rosette dishes: 3 cm.; sauce boats: 18
cm.; salad bowls: 10 cm.; vases: 15.5 cm. and 20.8 cm.

Inv. No.s PDMP 546-2658-f

All items are decorated with large, stylized, relief cabbage leaves; edges of the leaves are outlined with blue
and gold shading; on the leaves and between them are
bouquets of flowers. Items of a service with the pattern "cabbage leaves," manufactured at the Sevres
porcelain factory in 1760–1780, served as a model for
the painting of these. This service was intended for
formal dinners. Ordered in 1847, it was manufactured
during 1848–1853. It was intended to serve 250 people
and included more than 5500 items. Prominent
painters who worked on the service were E. Maximov
and A. Krasovsky.

— 294 —

ITEMS FROM THE "PRIGOROD"
("COUNTRY") FACETED GLASS SERVICE

For 12 persons.

3 FRUIT VASES, 12 WINE GLASSES,
12 CHAMPAGNE GLASSES, 12 RHINE WINE
GLASSES (GREEN), 12 WATER GLASSES, 12 SMALL
MUGS FOR MACEDOINE (A DISH OF BOILED
VEGETABLES AND/OR FRUITS WITH SAUCE),
12 VODKA GLASSES, 6 DECANTERS

1823.

Petersburg, Russia.

Imperial Glass Factory.

According to designs by I. A. Ivanov.

Cut crystal.

H. of vases: 31.3 and 55.5 cm.; of wine glasses: 13.5 cm.; of
champagne glasses: 17 cm.; of white wine glasses: 10.5 cm.; of
glasses: 7 cm.; of mugs: 7 cm.; of vodka glasses: 8.5 cm.; of decanters:
20, 26.5, 27.5, 23, 27.3, and 23 cm.

Inv. No.s PDMP 874-2189-st

Crystal items of the "Prigorod" ("Country") Faceted
Service were used together with the Banquet Service.
This crystal was made in 1823 at the Imperial Glass
Factory, by order of the Court administration. The
service included a large number of segmented fruit
vases which served to beautify the tables. The service
was used together with porcelain services during ceremonial receptions at Peterhof.

— 295 —

TABLE FORKS AND KNIVES

1870.

Village of Bachi, Vladimir Province, Russia.

Factory of Dmitri Kondratov (active from 1850s—1870s).

Steel, gilding, burnishing, etching; porcelain,
multicolored painting.

L. 24.8 cm. (knives); L. 20 cm. (forks).

On the metal, a stamp: "Kondratov Factory in Vachi village 1870"
and depiction of the coat of arms of Russia.

Inv. No.s PDMP 1682-1693-mt (knives); 1694-1705-mt (forks).

For 12 persons. Knife blades decorated with gold and
burnished ornament on an etched background; porcelain hafts with wildflowers painted on a pink ground;
forks with four tines and matching porcelain hafts.

Depiction of the coat of arms of Russia on the
items indicates that the factory was an official purveyor to the Imperial Court.

— 296 —

CRYSTAL ITEMS

serving 8, matching the Ropsha service.

8 WINE GLASSES, 8 WATER GLASSES,
8 CHAMPAGNE GLASSES, 3 DECANTERS
AND A PITCHER

1820s.

Petersburg, Russia.

Imperial Glass Factory.

H. of wine glasses: 9.8 cm.; of water glasses: 9 and 7 cm.;
of champagne glasses: 17 cm.; of decanters: 26 and 21.5 cm.;
of pitcher: 28 cm.

Inv. No.s PDMP 1998-2638-st

— 297 —

ITEMS OF THE ROPSHA SERVICE

For 8 persons.

8 SOUP PLATES, 8 FLAT PLATES, 8 DESSERT
PLATES, 4 SALAD BOWLS, 2 PLATTERS, 2 CANDY
BOWLS, WINEGLASS BUCKET, 2 SAUCER-PLATES,
3 FRUIT VASES, 2 CANDELABRA

Petersburg, Russia.

Imperial Porcelain Factory.

Porcelain, monochromatic covering over glaze,
gilding, ornamental cutting.

D. of soup plates: 23.5 cm.; of flat plates: 24 cm.;
of dessert plates: 22 cm.; H. of round salad bowls: 10.7 cm.;
of oval salad bowls: 10 cm.; D. of platters: 43.5 cm.; H. of candy
dishes: 19.2 cm.; of wineglass bucket: 15 cm.; D. of saucer-plates:
25.2 cm.; H. of vases: 47 and 40.5 cm.; of candelabra: 73 cm.

Marks of Nicholas I and Nicholas II period.

Inv. No.s PDMP 957-4210-f

On a blue background, gold ornament of palmettos
and lotus blossoms and a golden two-headed eagle under a crown.

The service was manufactured in 1823–1827. It
was originally intended for use at the Winter Palace in
Petersburg. It was designed for 50 people and in 1857
it was expanded to serve 80. In the second half of the
19th century the set was augmented by a tea service.
After 1853, part of the service was transferred to the
Ropsha Palace near Peterhof, whence it received its
name, "Ropshinsky." Sculptural aspects of the vases
were executed according to models by S. Pimenov.

— 298 —

TABLE CENTERPIECE

1800–1825.

Paris, France.

P. F. Tomir

Bronze, wood, gilding, mirrored glass.

H. 17 cm.

Inv. No. PDMP 2509-mt

Oval, with mirrored tray and openwork edges, depicting a bacchic procession.

— 299 —

TABLE KNIVES AND FORKS

1845–1855.

Zlatoust, Ural Mountains, Russia.

Zlatoust Factory.

Steel, jasper, etching, gilding.

L. 25.9 cm. (knives); L. 21.8 cm. (forks).

Engraved on blade: "Zlatoust".

Inv. No.s PDMP 1826-1831-mt (knives); 1832-1837-mt (forks).

For 6 persons. Knife blades of steel with gilded plant ornament on an etched ground; hafts of gray-green jasper; forks with three tines; matching jasper hafts.

TEA SERVICE

For 4 persons.

TEAPOT, SUGAR BOWL, CREAM PITCHER,
RINSE BOWL, 4 CUPS WITH SAUCERS

1863.

Petersburg, Russia.

Imperial Porcelain Factory.

Porcelain, multicolored painting over glaze, gilding.

Green marks under glaze: A II under a crown.

H. of teapot: 15 cm.; of sugar bowl: 11 cm.;
of cream pitcher: 12 cm.; of rinse bowl: 7.7 cm.;
of cups: 7.5 cm.; D. of saucers: 15.5 cm.

Inv. No.s PDMP 3628/1, 2-3631/1, 2; 3633-3636-f

Porcelain dyed pale green; over the surface, relief multicolored raspberry branches.

FOUR TEASPOONS

1894–1896.

Moscow, Russia.

Matryona Andreeva (owner of company from 1890–1908).

Silver, filigree, gilding, enamel.

L. 14 cm.

Inv. No. PDMP 368-371-dm

Decorated with multicolored enamel on filigree drawing.

COFFEE SERVICE

For 6 persons.

COFFEE POT, SUGAR BOWL,
6 CUPS WITH SAUCERS

1832–1838.

Petersburg, Russia.

Factory of S. Batenin.

Porcelain, multicolored painting over glaze, gilding.

Marks in porcelain: S.3.K.B.

H. of coffee pot: 22 cm.; of sugar bowl: 13.4 cm.;
of cups: 9.1 cm.; D. of saucers: 14.5 cm.

Inv. No.s PDMP 6379, 6381-6388/1, 2-f

Dark blue with gold ornament and, in unpainted areas, multicolored paintings of bouquets of flowers.

SIX TEASPOONS

1882.

Moscow, Russia.

Antip Kuzmichev (active 1856–1897).

Silver, gilding, carving, engraving.

L. 17.8 cm.

Mark: Moscow, "AK", "1882", "84".

Inv. No. PDMP 817-822-dm.

Gilded, with craved ornament on bowl.

⇀ 304 ⇀

TEA SERVICE

For 6 persons.

TEAPOT, SUGAR BOWL, RINSE BOWL,
6 CUPS WITH SAUCERS, VASE

1832–1838.

Petersburg, Russia.

Factory of S. Batenin.

Porcelain, gold glaze, ornamental cutting,
multicolored painting over glaze.

Marks in porcelain: S.E.K.B.

H. of teapot: 21 cm.; of sugar bowl: 12.3 cm.;
of rinse bowl: 11.4 cm.; of cups: 9.8 cm.; D. of saucers: 15 cm.;
H. of vase: 28.7 cm.

Inv. No. PDMP 7983/1, 2-7986/1,2; 1989/
1, 2; 7990/1, 2; 7995-7997, 3592-f.

On a background of gold with cut ornament, multicolored depiction of scenes with Chinese people.

⇀ 305 ⇀

SAMOVAR-COFFEEPOT

First third of 19th century.

Russia.

Bronze, brass, ebony, patina, gilding.

H. 52.1 cm.

Inv. No. PDMP 2510-mt.

With two reservoirs for boiling water and coffee, on
three paw-legs; lid crowned with a figure of a swan.

— 306 —

SAMOVAR

1843–1858.

Petersburg, Russia.

V. Dubinin (active 1843–1858).

Copper, silver applique.

H. 47.5 cm.

On the face of the base, a stamped mark: "by Dubinin"; under it: "Ser. Border".

Inv. No. PDMP 2037-mt

In the shape of a vase: widening toward the top, it is decorated with spoons and a relief of stylized plant ornament.

— 307 —

TEA SERVICE: CREAM PITCHER, SUGAR BOWL, TEAPOT, COFFEEPOT

1835–1840.

Moscow, Russia.

V. Rosenstrauch (active 1829–second half of 1830s).

Copper, silver spplique, gilding, ivory.

H. 10.2; 11.3; 16.4; and 20.8 cm.

On the face of the base, mark: "Rosenstrauch" and coat of arms of Russia.

Inv. No. PDMP 1900-1903-mt

Turnip shape; spooned, flanged upper edges decorated with relief acanthus and palmettos of silver applique.

— 308 —

TRAY

1833–1856.

Moscow, Russia.

Feodor Oehme (active 1833–after 1856).

Copper, silver applique.

71 × 48 cm.

On upper surface, near handle, stamp: "Oehme."

Inv. No. PDMP 1387-mt.

Of rectangular shape, with two handles; along the edge, stamped border of plant motif.

EMPERORS OF RUSSIA
Reign of the Tsars

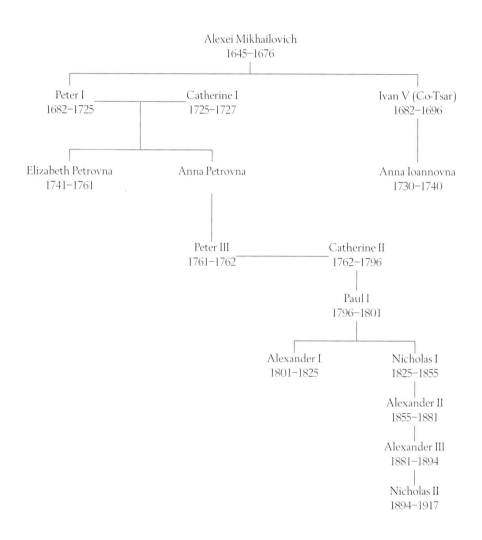

Alexei Mikhailovich
1645–1676

Peter I
1682–1725

Catherine I
1725–1727

Ivan V (Co-Tsar)
1682–1696

Elizabeth Petrovna
1741–1761

Anna Petrovna

Anna Ioannovna
1730–1740

Peter III
1761–1762

Catherine II
1762–1796

Paul I
1796–1801

Alexander I
1801–1825

Nicholas I
1825–1855

Alexander II
1855–1881

Alexander III
1881–1894

Nicholas II
1894–1917